PRISONER REENTRY AND
SOCIAL CAPITAL

June 7, 2010

Dear Jill:

PRISONER REENTRY AND SOCIAL CAPITAL

The Long Road to Reintegration

Thank you for
the many
opportunities you
gave us.
much appreciated.
Best wishes to your
future at Wake
Forest.
We deeply regret
we will not be
able to share
the success with
you + our colleagues
and friends.

Angela Hattery
and
Earl Smith

LEXINGTON BOOKS
A division of
ROWMAN & LITTLEFIELD PUBLISHERS, INC.
Lanham · Boulder · New York · Toronto · Plymouth, UK

Sincerely,
Earl

Published by Lexington Books
A division of Rowman & Littlefield Publishers, Inc.
A wholly owned subsidiary of The Rowman & Littlefield Publishing Group, Inc.
4501 Forbes Boulevard, Suite 200, Lanham, Maryland 20706
http://www.lexingtonbooks.com

Estover Road, Plymouth PL6 7PY, United Kingdom

British Library Cataloguing in Publication Information Available

Library of Congress Cataloging-in-Publication Data
Hattery, Angela.
  Prisoner reentry and social capital / Angela Hattery and Earl Smith.
    p. cm.
  Includes bibliographical references and index.
  ISBN 978-0-7391-4388-9 (cloth : alk. paper) – ISBN 978-0-7391-4389-6 (pbk. : alk.
paper) – ISBN 978-0-7391-4390-2 (electronic)
  1. Prisoners–Deinstitutionalization–United States. 2. Ex-convicts–Employment–United
States. 3. Social capital (Sociology)–United States. I. Smith, Earl, 1946- II. Title.
  HV9304.H38 2010
  365'.6470973–dc22   2010003884

Printed in the United States of America

To Emma and Travis: As you explore your own callings in life, may you always remember what you've learned from Darryl Hunt and the importance of "getting it right" and the problems for people like him when we don't. —Love, Mom

To Earl: Wow . . . working on this project took my breath away. No matter how much we had read about and prepared for these interviews, I was awestruck by the realities of lives filled with addiction, abuse, the trauma of prison and the struggles to reenter the "free world." As a woman and a mom I will never forget listening to Kezia talk about laboring to birth a child while in shackles. The image haunts me. Thank you for pushing us to complete the project even when the hurdles to doing so—from the IRB, from the prison personnel, lack of funding—were so high and seemingly insurmountable. As with everything, I never could have done this work with out and can't imagine even trying. You inspire me daily. —Angela

To Angela: Another one done! While never easy, these book projects—now numbering five—are a pleasure to research, write, and edit while working with you.

At the end of this journey and looking to relax I am reminded that there will be, I am sure, an e-mail that starts: "E. S. I have an idea for a book . . ." I eagerly await that e-mail. —E. S.

To all of our friends and contributors to this project, Tania, Emma, Travis, the dedicated reference staff at the Z. Smith Reynolds Library, Wake Forest University: THANK YOU. —Earl

Thank you to all the men and women who shared with such honesty their struggles with addiction, sexual abuse, incarceration, and reentry. We wish you all the best and dedicate this book to you. —Angela and Earl

Contents

Acknowledgments

A S WITH ALL BOOK PROJECTS, WE ARE GRATEFUL FOR THE HELP of many people, but we acknowledge that writing a book is a solitary process and we, the authors, take sole responsibility for any errors.

We owe a debt of gratitude to many people; first and foremost are those who helped us to conduct the research for this project. We are grateful to the staff of the Darryl Hunt Project for Freedom and Justice for providing us access to the men and women who are attempting to rebuild their lives after periods of incarceration. We are especially grateful to Darryl Hunt, who has always opened his doors and his life to us, and to Pam Peoples-Joyner, who identified individuals for interviews and who allowed us to "set up shop" in the office where we were able to conduct interviews in a private, comfortable setting.

We are grateful to Wake Forest Associate Provost for Research Mark Welker and Wake Forest Dean Paul Ribisl for providing the funding necessary to conduct the interviews and have the data transcribed. We are grateful to the research fund at Colgate University, which provided the funding for Colgate student Susan Fortkiewicz, who transcribed interviews and coded transcribed data.

We are grateful to Mrs. Tania Acuna for her help in taping interviews, transferring videotape material to electronic files, and organizing paperwork associated with the interviews. She even allowed her son Jean Carlo to assist as well. Thank you!

We are grateful to Travis Mathew Hattery Freetly and Emma Elise Hattery Freetly for their help in taping interviews and to Emma for transcribing interviews. We are grateful to Michael Porter for doing the research on drug treatment and for his and Emma's other assistance with the project including putting ditty bags together for the Darryl Hunt Project's summer Homecoming celebration.

We are grateful to Mr. Alan McLare, whose interest in this project opened up the door for its publication. Sadly, Mr. McLare passed away in late 2009 before this book entered production, but we owe him a debt of gratitude for his help with this project as well as two other book projects.

At Lexington Books we are grateful to Michael Sisskin, our acquisitions editor, for taking on this project and for the help Lindsey Schauer provided with the graphics. She transformed all of the figures and tables as well as assisted with cover design.

Primarily we are grateful to the men and women who opened up their lives to us and allowed us to understand more fully the struggles that men and women who are reentering the "free world" face. Their stories were often painful, sometimes humorous, and incredibly intimate. The opportunity to learn about the struggles of drug addiction, what it means to be a sex offender, and what it is like to give birth while incarcerated dramatically increased our understanding of the complexities of reentry and we are proud to be able to share these insights and theoretical framings with our readers.

Angela J. Hattery, PhD
Earl Smith, PhD
Winston-Salem, North Carolina
January 2010

1

Introduction to the Issue

Who Are Reentry Felons and Why Does This Matter?

At age 39, Terrence Brown has struggled with crack addiction and mental illness, and has no high school degree. Like nearly 40 percent of all black men in New York City, Brown is often unemployed. He could very well find himself in prison. And not for the first time, either. For the past decade, Brown has traveled the intractable circuit from jail, to the streets of Harlem, to jail again. (Chen 2007)

"If you do the crime you gotta do the time." This adage reflects the overall attitude most Americans have about crime and the criminal justice system. Implicit in this adage is the notion that once "the time" is done, the individual is free to reenter society and resume a normal life. This couldn't be farther from the truth. In fact, the vast majority of individuals who attempt to return to the "free world" after some period of incarceration face barriers that are often insurmountable, and for a variety of reasons, more than two-thirds eventually return back to prison, most within three years.

The average reader reflecting on the previous passage is probably not concerned about the revolving door of incarceration. Why should he or she be, especially if it does not affect him or her? We will demonstrate in this book that the average reader should care about this phenomenon because it is in his or her self-interest to do so, not necessarily because he or she will become part of this cycle or even have a close family member or friend who does. Rather, the average reader should care because what underlies the inability of individuals to successfully reenter the "free world" is the high probability that the ex-offender will return to engaging in criminal behavior during these periods in the "free world" and as a result we are all potential victims for their latest crimes.

An Illustration: The Jaycee Dugard Kidnapping Case

In 1991 Phillip Garrido kidnapped eleven-year-old Jaycee Dugard and held her as a sex slave in a series of tents in his backyard in El Dorado County, California, until August 2009, when she was discovered by the local sheriff eighteen years after her abduction. Garrido not only raped Dugard, but also fathered two children by her, who he also held hostage. When they were discovered in August 2009, the girls, who were eleven and fifteen, had lived their entire lives in backyard tents without electricity or running water. They had never been to school; they had never been off of Garrido's property. Every aspect of the case was stunning including the fact that it created hope for so many parents whose children have been missing for years.

Perhaps the saddest part of the case is the fact that Garrido was a repeat offender. In November of 1976 Garrido kidnapped and raped Katie Callaway Hall. Garrido held Hall for eight hours in a storage locker and repeatedly raped her. She gained her freedom when he left her alone for a short period of time and a patrolman noticed the lock on the storage unit appeared to have been tampered with. Hall heard the patrolman outside the locker and screamed for help. Though initially he believed Garrido's story that the two were a couple enjoying an evening of sexual frolicking, when Katie ran from the storage locker naked, the police officer took Garrido into custody. Garrido was sentenced to fifty years in prison, but served only ten. He was released in 1987 and by 1991, just four years later, he had kidnapped Dugard. This chilling case illustrates several key problems in the criminal justice system that we will address in this book, including the high rate of recidivism for sex offenders, and the risk that failed reentry poses to our public safety.

An Illustration: Police Officers Killed in Seattle, Washington

On Sunday, November 29, 2009, just three days after Thanksgiving, Maurice Clemmons shot and killed four police officers in Tacoma, Washington, as they sat in a neighborhood coffee shop drinking coffee and working on their laptops. This was one of the worst multiple homicides of law enforcement personnel in U.S. history. During the shooting, one of the officers got a shot off and injured Maurice Clemmons and a two-day "manhunt" ensued. After being helped by various family members and former associates he met in prison, his aunt turned him in to the police. Though the police didn't capture Clemmons based on the tips provided by his aunt, hours later an officer encountered a suspicious man attempting to fix a broken-down truck. When the officer saw the man's face he immediately recognized him as Clemmons. When Clemmons refused to stop and put his hands up the officer shot and killed him. The events of these three days paralyzed the Seattle/Tacoma area as citizens lived in fear of the "police shooter." And, though Clemmons's death certainly brought some relief, his story unfolded in to a different kind of nightmare: the failure of the criminal justice system.

As the tragedy in Tacoma was unfolding, it didn't take long for journalists to uncover two important aspects of Clemmons's life: (1) that he had a long criminal record and had spent most his adult life in prison and (2) that systems along the way had broken down such that Clemmons, like Garrido, had been released from prison on more than one occasion after serving significantly less than his full sentence. In fact, just a week and a half before his shooting rampage he had been released from jail after he was finally allowed to post bail after a judge dropped a fugitive warrant for his arrest in Arkansas.

Clemmons's story is far too complex to analyze fully here, but some key details are important to understanding recidivism as a threat to pubic safety. Clemmons grew up poor in the racially turbulent, economically depressed Mississippi Delta region of Arkansas. At the age of sixteen Clemmons, having moved with his mother and five siblings to Little Rock, Arkansas, in pursuit of a better life, went on a seven-month crime spree that included robbing and assaulting a woman, burglarizing the home of a state trooper, and bringing a pistol to school. At age seventeen he was sentenced to 108 years in prison. His family and others felt that Clemmons was the victim of a racist, southern criminal justice system that handed down a sentence more suited to those convicted of "rape or murder" (*Seattle Times* 2009). Eleven years later, after twice being denied parole by the Arkansas parole board, and after a history of violent behavior in prison—including sexual assault, physical assault, and selling drugs—then-governor Mike Huckabee agreed. "Huckabee granted the request [for clemency] in May 2000, citing Clemmons's youth when the crimes were committed. . . . His decision in the spotlight, Huckabee said he was influenced by Arkansas' history of disproportionate sentences for poor black men" (*Seattle Times* 2009).

Hoping to escape the violence and start over, Clemmons moved to the Seattle area where many of his relatives had settled beginning in the 1970s (*Seattle Times* 2009). Though he was able to hold some legitimate jobs, he couldn't seem to stay out of trouble. In 2001 he was convicted of armed robbery, again in Arkansas, and served three years in prison before being released in 2004. Clemmons moved back to the Seattle area, married Nicole Smith, and based on evidence collected after his death, was involved in selling drugs and real estate scams (*Seattle Times* 2009). By early 2009 things had begun to spiral out of control and he was arrested and charged with eight separate felony counts, including the rape of a child—his twelve-year-old step-daughter. He was arrested in early July and based on the prosecutor's arguments his bail for these charges was set relatively high—she argued that facing his "third strike" he was a flight risk. Even had Clemmons been able to raise bail for these charges, he was denied the opportunity to post bail and was required to be held in custody because of a fugitive warrant against him in Arkansas (*Seattle Times* 2009). According to the reports in the *Seattle Times*, his wife Nicole, whose daughter he was accused of molesting, worked relentlessly for his release. Among other tactics, she attempted to withdraw the molestation claim, and eventually she wrote to a judge in Arkansas and pleaded to get the fugitive warrant rescinded. She was successful, and on November 23, 2009, just six days before the rampage, Clemmons was allowed to post bail and he was released from the Pierce County jail. Family and friends report that over Thanksgiving he talked about killing cops and children, and perhaps because he feared the life sentence that would accompany a third felony conviction or perhaps because he was mentally unstable, on Sunday, November 29, 2009, he opened fire on four police officers in a coffee shop in his home neighborhood, killing them all (*Seattle Times* 2009).

How did all of this happen and what went so wrong? There are no easy answers to this inquiry, but the research done by the staff of the *Seattle Times* and reported there makes clear that warning signs were ignored; a mental health evaluation done in October 2009 while he was in jail found Clemmons to be a threat to public safety but not a significant enough threat to warrant his commitment to a psychiatric hospital. Decisions about Clemmons's release from prison and the decision to rescind a warrant that allowed him to post bail were made, it seems, without full consideration of the circumstances. And just like Garrido and so many others, Clemmons was released back in to the "free world" without enough supervision to ensure that he would not threaten public safety. Of course hindsight is twenty-twenty but both cases presented here illustrate not only the fact that recidivism is a significant concern to those who work in the criminal justice system but also that it should be a concern to all of us who live in the "free world" and are the potential victims of the next crime.

Recidivism: An Overview

Among the many issues and problems identified by scholars and critics of the criminal justice system is the "revolving door" concept that characterizes our prison system in the United States. Early criminologists and penologists conceptualized prisons in the following ways: (1) as institutions that segregated individuals who were too dangerous to live among the citizenry, (2) as a system for punishment—namely removing privileges as consequences for deviant behavior, and (3) as a system with deterrent qualities—those criminals who were not too dangerous to reenter society would refrain from further criminal behavior because they would not want to return to prison. Additionally, most early criminologists and penologists also assumed that the deterrent effect would influence the rest of the citizenry from engaging in deviant behavior (Sykes 2007). The beliefs early criminologists held about the harshness of prison led them to conclude that prison would deter future deviance and thus recidivism would be a minor concern.

Today, one of the most pressing issues facing scholars, those who work in the criminal justice system and the citizenry as a whole, is the extraordinarily high rate of recidivism. Recidivism is a problem for a variety of reasons, including the fact that it alone accounts for a significant percentage of prison entries each year. According to the Bureau of Justice Statistics, in 2004, 1.12 million individuals were sentenced to state prison. With a recidivism rate of nearly 70 percent in three years, we can conclude that 20–30 percent of prison entries in a given year are the result of recidivism.

Recidivism Statistics

Each year during the twenty-first century the number of individuals being released back in to the "free world" has grown such that by 2010 estimates are that nearly 750,000 people—three-quarters of a million—will be release from prison or jail (Bureau of Justice Statistics; Petersilia 2000, 2003). The recidivism rate is calculated across the three-year period after release. This three-year recidivism rate is calculated to be 67 percent.[1] Thus, of the 650,000 individuals who will be released in 2009 (Bureau of Justice Statistics), nearly half a million will return to prison by 2012. In other words, the majority of men and women who exit prison will ultimately be unsuccessful in their attempts to reenter the "free world."

Gender makes some difference: men recidivate at 60–65 percent, and women at 52 percent.[2] Mild race differences persist as well: within three years, 60–65 percent of African Americans, 59 percent of Whites, and 49 percent of Hispanics return to prison.[3] Almost everyone studying recidivism knows that within approximately three years, seven in ten formerly incarcerated individuals will have been rearrested and returned to prison, either for a new crime or for violating conditions of their most recent release (Freudenberg, Daniels et al. 2005).

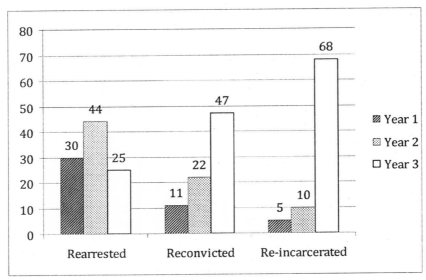

FIGURE 1.1
Recidivism of Released Prisoners (1994), Bureau of Justice Statistics

Barriers to Reentry

One of the most pressing issues, then, is understanding better the predictors of recidivism and thus, by definition, the barriers that make successful reentry difficult and unsuccessful. The majority of scholars and research that focuses on recidivism is based on examining overall rates of recidivism for different populations. As noted above, gender and race both play a role in predicting recidivism, as does length of sentence and type of conviction. For example, drug offenders and sexual offenders have excessively high rates of recidivism whereas those convicted of homicide have remarkably low rates of recidivism. Despite understanding who is most likely to recidivate, we know very little about why people recidivate and we know even less about the particular barriers that individuals face that shape the likelihood of recidivism. This book fills this gap by focusing on the reentry experiences of twenty-five men and women who shared with us their own experiences with the difficult process of reentering the "free world." In sum, we confirmed, as others have shown, that there are several key factors that influence reentry, including race, socio-economic status prior to incarceration, sobriety, employment, and access to stable housing. However, we discovered a key factor that has been relatively ignored in the literature on recidivism and reentry: social capital. Though we devote an entire chapter—chapter 2—to a discussion of social capital and its influence on the reentry process, we note here that in short, when men and women exiting prison have support networks that provide access to information about housing and employment, or can even provide references for apartment leasing or employment, individuals with an otherwise grim prognosis for successful reentry were able to overcome the struggles to reentry and successfully become productive members of their local communities.

Prison Population/Rates of Incarceration

In order to better understand the importance of recidivism and the colossal barriers to reentry, we provide an overview of the context in which these processes occur: the state of incarceration in the United States. The rate of incarceration in the United States has increased steadily since 1980, primarily due to the inception of felony drug laws and "Three Strikes You're Out" laws. In the last few years, the rate has been especially steep, notably for African Americans and, to a lesser extent, Hispanics. In 2008, more than 2.3 million Americans (0.7 percent of the U.S. population) were incarcerated, in nearly 1,700 state, federal, and private prisons, and more than 5 million Americans were under other forms of custodial supervision, including probation and parole, for a total of 7.2 million Americans—3.2 percent of the U.S. population—under some form of custodial or supervisory control of the criminal justice system.[4]

The United States incarcerates a greater percentage of its population (nearly 1 percent) than any other industrialized country in the world (Elsner 2006) (see figure 1.2). As a point of reference, the United States incarcerates more of its citizens on drug convictions alone than the entire incarcerated population of the European Union, which has a population significantly greater than ours (Elsner 2006; Western 2006). And, if predictions hold, the recession will result in even higher rates of incarceration (Rozas 2008).

This addiction to incarceration carries with it many problems, including significant race and social class disparities, wrongful convictions, one of the highest rates of capital punishment in the world (Hattery and Smith 2008) and one of the highest rates of sentencing juveniles to life sentences.

As important as all of these problems are to social scientists, social justice activists, and reformers, these problems are relatively confined to small subsets of the U.S. population and are invisible to many if not most Americans.

This over-reliance on incarceration creates another problem that touches all communities: prisoner reentry. Despite having the highest rates of life sentences and death row sentences in the world, the overwhelming majority of the more than 2.2 million Americans who are incarcerated on any given day

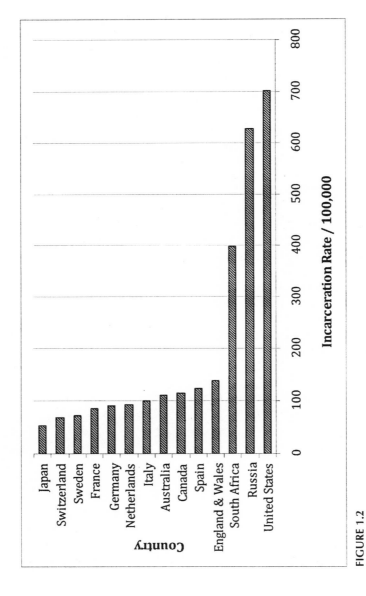

FIGURE 1.2
Incarceration Rates by Country, Mauer 2003

TABLE 1.1
U.S. Prison Population by Race and Gender
Compared to the U.S. Population by Race and Gender

Race/Gender	U.S. Population	U.S Prison Population	Ratio
White Men	120,326,022	600,000	0.5%
White Women	122,313,220	314,127	0.2%
African American Women	20,419,202	673,773	3.2%
African American Men	18,639,632	1.1 million	5.4%

will be released from prison and return, most likely, to the communities from which they came (Petersilia 2003).

The data presented in table 1.1 summarize the make-up of both the U.S. population as a whole and the prison population specifically. The data indicate that in the United States, on any given day, 5 percent of all African American men are incarcerated, compared to only 0.5 percent of their White counterparts. In other words, African American men are *ten times* more likely to be incarcerated than White men. Not surprisingly, women are far less likely to be incarcerated than are men, and this holds across racial identity. Yet, race differences also persist across gender, such that African American women are more likely to be incarcerated than are their White counterparts. It is interesting to note, however, that the racial gap for women is significantly narrower than for men.

As demonstrated in figure 1.3, though African American men make up approximately 6 percent of the U.S. population, they make up nearly half (43

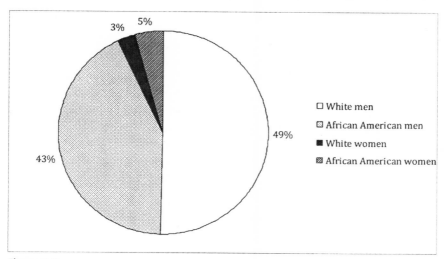

Figure 1.3
U.S. Prison Population by Race and Gender

TABLE 1.2
Probability of Incarceration for Women (Harrison 2004)

- 11 out of every 1,000 women will be incarcerated in their lifetimes:
  - 5 out of every 1,000 White women
  - 36 out of every 1,000 African American women

percent) of the prison population; in other words, African American men make up more of the U.S. prison population than White men, and all women, combined.

As shocking as these data are, the probability of incarceration over the lifetime of individual men and women is even more severe. The data in tables 1.2 and 1.3 compare the probability for incarceration by race and gender. Over their lifetimes, nearly *one-third of African American men will spend time in prison.*

It is in this context that prisoner reentry and recidivism must be explored. For example, when we extrapolate rates of incarceration by race to individual communities, we note that individuals returning from prison to the "free world" face very different circumstances. For example, low-income African American men and women return from prison to communities where as many as 50 percent of the men have been or will be incarcerated. Coupled with low rates of homeownership and high rates of unemployment, the barriers that African American men and women face to successful reentry are significantly greater than those faced by their White counterparts. It is precisely these issues that we will explore in this book.

The Interviews

During the summer of 2008 we conducted in-depth interviews with twenty-five men and women who were attempting to reenter the "free world" after periods of incarceration. Reflective of the U.S. prison population as a whole, of the twenty-five individuals we interviewed, only two were women and only three were White, one was Hispanic, and the remaining twenty-one were African American.

The interviews, which frequently lasted two hours, were essentially mini–life histories (Shaw 1930) that focused on subjects' families of orientation, history of "deviance," pathways to prison, and experiences with reentry. Some

TABLE 1.3
Probability of Incarceration for Men (Harrison 2004)

- 90 out of every 1,000 men will be incarcerated in their lifetimes:
  - 44 out of every 1,000 White men
  - 285 out of every 1,000 African American men

had only been to prison once, while others had cycled in and out. Some had served only a year or two whereas others had served more than thirty-five years (not always continuously) in prison.

Among other things, our interviews provide a deeper and more precise understanding of the biases faced by reentry felons[5] in the labor market. Most interviewees shared discouraging stories of applying for job after job, yet many not only were employed but also had secured many different jobs across the different periods when they were not locked up. This discrepancy held across race, gender, class, length of conviction, and type of conviction. For example, Lindell, a sixty-year-old African American man released several months prior to the interview, having served nearly twenty years in federal prison for drugs and weapons charges, was able to get a job cooking in a local chain restaurant. Though he seems to have nearly every strike against him, his relationship to a key member of a reentry program, who vouched for his employability, allowed him to beat the odds. In contrast, Sammy, another sixty-year-old African American man who has served a total of more than thirty years in prison—constituted by a series of four- or five-year sentences—continues to be unemployed nearly a year after release. What is the difference? One key difference is that Sammy is among the ranks of the chronically homeless. Without a social capital network on which to draw, he has neither housing nor employment. Other interviewees who were able to find jobs had family members or close friends who had influence in hiring decisions. One example is JB, whose friend, a manager at a fast-food restaurant, hired him after he had served several years in prison. This relationship compensated for JB's felony record, which includes convictions for drug possession, providing a minor with drugs, kidnapping, and indecent liberties with a minor. Finally, a Hispanic subject, Tito, argued that the only way he could get a job was if he knew someone who owned a company. His perspective was based on the fact that he had been unable to get a job after he was released from prison and relocated to North Carolina to live with his mother. In contrast, previously, after serving several prison terms of three to five years, after which he was released to his home city, Miami, where many Hispanics—several of whom were his acquaintances—owned small businesses, he was always able to find employment.

What This Book Will Do

This book takes as its starting point the experiences of the twenty-five men and women we interviewed during the summer of 2008 about their experiences with reentering the "free world" after a period of incarceration. Analyzing the experiences of these men and women provides the structure of the book. Specifically, the chapters of this book are organized around the primary themes that emerged from our analysis. We begin the discussion by focusing in depth on the factors that inhibit successful reentry and utilize the stories from the interviews to illustrate successes and failures. Next we examine individual characteristics that inhibit successful reentry: addiction (chapter 3) and sex offender status (chapter 4). Moving on to more macro-level factors, we devote an entire chapter, chapter 5, to the unique challenges that women face in terms of incarceration and reentry. Following our discussion of gender, we turn our attention in chapter 6 to a focused discussion on the role that social capital plays in prisoner reentry. We chose to devote an entire chapter to the relationship between social capital and prisoner reentry because it is a factor that has been relatively ignored by other researchers and yet emerged as one of the most important factors that shaped the reentry experience. For example, in some cases in our study, the unusually high rates of recidivism associated with the experiences of African American men with lengthy sentences and multiple episodes of incarceration were overcome by their access to *specific social capital networks*. In chapter 7 we explore one of the most distressing aspects of incarceration: wrongful conviction and exoneration. In this chapter, we depart from relying exclusively on the interview data and provide a statistical analysis on the small number of exonerations that have occurred in the United States since 1989. We couple this analysis with an in-depth discussion of the experiences of a single exoneree: Mr. Darryl Hunt. Finally, we conclude the book, in chapter 8, with a summary of the findings presented as well as some suggestions for addressing the key barriers ex-inmates face as they attempt to successfully reenter the "free world" and become productive citizens and family members.

Notes

1. www.ojp.usdoj.gov/bjs/reentry/recidivism.htm (accessed on September 6, 2009).

2. www.ojp.usdoj.gov/bjs/reentry/characteristics.htm (accessed on September 10, 2009).

3. www.ojp.usdoj.gov/bjs/reentry/characteristics.htm (accessed on September 10, 2009).

4. Justice Policy Institute, 2000; www.justicepolicy.org/images/upload/00-05_REP_PunishingDecade_AC.pdf (accessed on September 6, 2009).

5. We use the term "reentry felons" to draw attention to the fact that first and foremost one's status as a convict is what sociologists call a "master status." In other words, long after the term of one's incarceration, the status of "convict" sticks with individuals much as their race/ethnicity or gender significantly shapes their lives; one cannot then really be an "ex" convict. Including the term "felon" distinguishes these men and women from those exiting jail without a felony conviction. Because so many of the barriers to reentry turn on a felony, this is an important distinction.

2

Barriers to Reentry
and Increased Recidivism

I used to go out every day. My day started like 6:30. I hopped on the bus. I would go around and fill out applications all day long, up until about 2 or 3 o'clock in the evening. That was a job in itself. And each time, because of my record, it was like, "No"—that's what I'm thinking that "No, no, no, no, no." I just got tired of it. And then, when you do this for like so long, you get burned out.

—William

The main concern is not to go to work at McDonalds. I mean they say, "Oh go to work at McDonalds." Well, McDonald's is not even hiring an ex-convict.

—Tito

RESEARCH SUGGESTS THAT IN 2010 nearly three-quarters of a million people—mostly men and disproportionately African American and Hispanic men—will return to communities all over the United States (Travis 2005). In just the county in which we conducted this research (Forsyth, North Carolina) we expect at least 1,200 people to be released from prison before the end of 2010—into a community of less than 200,000 people—or 0.6 percent of the county's population.

Though the common belief among Americans is that everyone deserves a second chance, especially after an individual has paid for his or her crime, the reality is that successful reentry is difficult at best and elusive for most. And, though some may argue that this is nothing to worry about because it simply amounts to more punishment for an individual who made bad choices, the reality is that barriers to reentry significantly shape the probability for recidivism—which as noted in the previous chapter, is approximately 70 percent in three years—and recidivism is a problem that affects all individuals and communities. Furthermore, recidivism is a major contributor to the overall size of the prison population; if we can reduce recidivism we can significantly reduce incarceration rates (Newman 2008).

Barriers to Reentry

The majority of this chapter will be devoted to outlining the significant and structural barriers to successful reentry that reentry felons face, the barriers that men and women experience as they attempt to remake their lives on the outside. But, before we outline the barriers and examine people's lived experiences in navigating these barriers, we must raise a question about incarceration that seldom is raised: does the United States actively work to promote reentry or do in fact government and big businesses have a vested interested in over-incarceration, thereby favoring high rates of recidivism as this is the largest contributor to the burgeoning prison population?

As we have argued elsewhere (Hattery and Smith 2008), there are several institutions—namely the government and multinational corporations—that have a vested interest in *not* reducing rates of incarceration or fostering successful reentry, but rather in maintaining and even growing the prison system in the United States. We base this argument on three key issues: (1) the relationship between unemployment and incarceration, (2) the use of prisons as a strategy to cordon off the underclass and (3) the relationship between prisons and multinational corporations or what we term the "Prison Industrial Complex" or PIC.

Unemployment and Incarceration

Chang and Thompkins (2002) track the relationship between unemployment and incarceration. They note that across the entire twentieth century, rates of unemployment and incarceration are positively correlated: namely that when unemployment goes up, sentencing laws get adjusted such that incarceration rates go up, and when unemployment plummets, so do incarceration rates. How do they make sense of this intriguing finding? They provide at least two reasons for such a strong correlation between unemployment rates and incarceration rates:

(1) First because incarcerated people are *not* counted against the unemployment rates, one way to artificially reduce the official unemployment rate is to incarcerate a portion of the population that is most likely to be unemployed.[1]

(2) Second because incarceration removes competition in tight labor markets, especially the sectors that rely most heavily on low-skilled and de-skilled workers, which are precisely the sectors in the U.S. economy where we see the highest levels of unemployment and layoffs, especially during the recession of the first decade of the twenty-first century. The population most likely to be incarcerated—those with little human capital—are precisely the same people who would be competing for increasingly scarce jobs. By incarcerating a disproportionate number of African American men with few skills, the competition in these tight labor markets is reduced (see Chang and Thompkins 2002; Hattery and Smith 2008).

Incarceration as a Tool for Cordoning off the Under Class

Social theorists Erik Olin Wright and Loic Wacquant have argued that the U.S. capitalist economy is bogged down by inefficiency. One source of inefficiency is individuals with very low human capital and thus few skills to sell in the labor market. Both scholars acknowledge the growing "under class"—individuals who don't graduate from high school, have few skills that are useful in a capitalist post-industrial economy, and are otherwise a "burden" to capitalism. Both argue that the under class has been ghettoized—both in urban ghettos and in rural areas, particularly in the Deep South (Hattery and Smith 2007). These urban and rural ghettos are characterized by high levels of unemployment—often topping 65 percent—low levels of education, and no industry. Capitalists don't build factories and small businesses don't open in either urban or rural ghettos. This results in a huge chasm between mainstream America and the under class; the under class is effectively cordoned off—out of sight and mind—of middle America thus allowing capitalism to churn along more efficiently (Wright 1997).[2]

Wright (1997) and Wacquant (2001) go on to suggest that prisons are another strategy or location that capitalists and the government can utilize to cordon off the under class. Prisons become warehouses for the poor (Elsner 2006), those addicted to drugs and alcohol, those who are mentally unstable, and those who have been unable amass the human capital necessary to obtain and maintain sustainable employment (Haney and Zimbardo 1998). Thus, as long as there remains an under class—and in the current economy it is likely to grow—there will be significant reasons for those in power to continue to warehouse the under class far away from the gaze of middle America; and prisons provide a suitable, perhaps even ideal,[3] location.

The Prison Industrial Complex (PIC)

Finally, as we argue elsewhere (Hattery and Smith 2008), the growing relationship between prisons and industry—the prison industrial complex—creates a high demand for incarceration. Specifically, members of the under class that Wright (1997) and Wacquant (2001) describe are suddenly transformed from unexploitable labor into exploitable labor by a variety of multinational corporations ranging from airline companies to McDonalds to Microsoft to Starbucks to Victoria's Secret that contract with prisons to provide manufacturing labor and service labor, including medical transcription, staffing customer service "call centers" for airlines to the manufacturing labor necessary to produce products ranging from Nintendo "game cubes" to Victoria's Secret lingerie. As more and more labor is demanded by capitalism there is an increasing demand for incarcerated individuals whose labor can be easily exploited. We note this development is also fueled by the continuing growth of the private prison corporations (Hallett 2004).

Why would corporations employ prisoners? *Cheap labor!* Our analysis shows that there are no OSHA laws to abide by, and also when the work slows down workers can be "laid off" by simply sending them back to their cells without severance packages or concerns about unemployment benefits, and there are no health insurance or retirement benefits to pay; on average inmates are paid far less than minimum wage—anywhere from fifty cents to a few dollars a *day*, depending on the type of jail or prison in which they are incarcerated and depending on the labor contracts negotiated by the corporations.

Furthermore we argue that prison industries create an attractive alternative to out-sourcing and off-shoring that allows manufacturing companies to compete in tight profit markets by taking advantage of low-wage/no benefits labor while continuing to proclaim proudly that their product is still *Made in America*. The low labor costs allow companies to net enormous profits on a magnitude consistent with those who choose to have their products manufactured in developing nations like Singapore (Hattery and Smith 2008).

Thus, the fundamental question becomes, what is the relationship between the interests that the government and big businesses have in high rates of incarceration and the barriers that prisoners face to successful reentry? As the reader will see, when we consider the role that the government in particular plays in setting up barriers to reentry we return to the same question: does the

United States actively work to promote reentry or do in fact government and big businesses have a vested interested in over-incarceration, thereby favoring high rates of recidivism as this is the largest contributor to the burgeoning prison population?

Employment and Housing

Two of the most pressing problems facing reentry felons—those men and women reentering society with a felony conviction—are employment and housing (Petersilia 2003; Visher, LaVigne et al. 2004). Clearly, employment and stable housing are critical elements to the success of *all individuals and families.* And, critical to both is the fact that housing and employment form a sort of "feedback loop"; it is difficult if not impossible to keep a stable home when one is unemployed and it is difficult and often impossible to keep a job when one is homeless. Thus, the success in obtaining one is inextricably linked to the success in obtaining the other.

Though much of the research on homelessness (Bloom 2005) documents many of the problems of seeking a job when one is homeless—such as the lack of a permanent address or phone number to list on applications where potential employers can contact a job-seeker to the stigma associated with listing a homeless shelter as one's address—we learned from many of the men we interviewed that there are other barriers as well, specifically the fact that most homeless shelters have a curfew, a time by which all residents must be checked-in, typically 7 pm. Yet, many of the jobs that the homeless and reentry felons in particular are eligible for involve factory and warehouse work that is done around the clock—three shifts are operating daily. Based on principles like "last hired, first fired," the reentry felons we interviewed noted that often they were only offered those jobs that were second or third shift. Taking a job during the second or third shift meant missing the curfew at the homeless shelter and jeopardizing one's housing arrangement. Thus, the catch-22s of housing and employment and the feedback loop between them went far deeper than other researchers or we ourselves anticipated. We turn now to a discussion of the specific barriers that reentry felons face to securing employment and stable housing.

Employment Bans

A felony record creates an enormous barrier to employment (Pager 2003; 2007). This is especially true for African American men. Specifically, Pager's experiment documented that when male "testers" applied for employment, White men were more likely, overall, to be offered a "call back" than African American men; White men without a felony were the most likely to be offered a call back; but most disturbing, *White men with a felony were more likely to be offered a call back than African American men without a felony.* Only 3 percent of African American men posing as "testers with a felony record" were offered a call back. This study illustrates the severity of the impact on employment opportunities that African American men with felony convictions face (Pager 2003; 2007).

In addition to the discrimination they face with potential employers, they also face bans on certain types of jobs and employment certificates. Mukamal's (2004) research notes:

> Employers in most states can deny jobs to people who were arrested but *never convicted* of any crime. . . . Employers in a growing number of professions are barred by state licensing agencies from hiring people with a wide range of criminal convictions, even convictions which are unrelated to the job or license sought. (10)

To make matters worse, Mukamal notes that some of the licensing bans apply to trades that inmates are taught in prison as part of rehabilitation programs. For example, she notes that many prisons offer inmates the chance to certify in

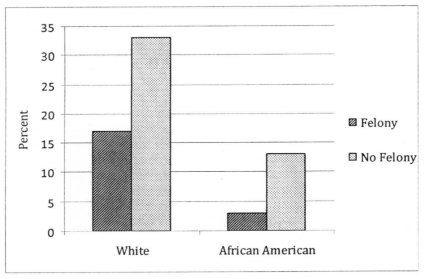

FIGURE 2.1
Devah Pager, (2003), "The Mark of a Criminal Record." *American Journal of Sociology* **108:937–75.**

barbering, but most states ban individuals with a felony record from holding a barber's license (Mukamal 2004). Thus, there is a huge disconnect between the skills prisons invest in teaching to inmates and the jobs they will be able to obtain once they reenter the free world. This finding seriously draws in to question the professed rehabilitation goal of state corrections departments.

Countless men we interviewed who had spent any reasonable length of time in prison (more than five years) talked at length about the various certification programs they had completed, partly as a way to fill time and partly as a way to prepare—they thought and were told—for their reentry. Bill's experiences were echoed by many. Bill had spent his time in prison pursuing training and certifications in the trades: construction, electrical wiring, plumbing, and so forth. Well equipped with his certificates, when Bill was released from prison he immediately started applying for jobs in the construction industry. Potential employers were usually impressed with his credentials, but questions arose when they looked at his certificates and noticed that all were earned at places with names like: Morrisville State Institutional Facility. When they inquired where exactly his certificates were earned, Bill had to admit that he had earned them as an inmate in a state prison. Suddenly the once-interested employer no longer had a need to hire in Bill's areas of expertise. This simple but critical illustration was experienced perhaps hundreds of times by the men we interviewed. We can only surmise how frustrating it is to commit to the types of training these certificates require, all along believing they are your "ticket" to a better life post-prison, only to find them discarded by potential employers who are more worried about the felonies and incarceration than the skills one developed.

Social Welfare Bans

In addition to the disenfranchisement and barriers to employment that reentry felons face, as part of the 1996 TANF reform and the changing drug laws of the 1980s and 1990s,[4] which we will discuss at length in chapter 3, a series of bans were imposed on reentry felons that prevent them from accessing many of the social programs that provide basic support. Proponents of these bans argue that they work as a crime deterrent by operating as an incentive to keep young people out of the kinds of trouble that will result in a felony, especially involvement with drugs. Opponents of these bans argue that denying reentry felons, particularly individuals with felony drug convictions, access to social welfare programs that provide housing, income support, and educational support amounts to stacking the deck against people who, without these support programs, will not be able to successfully reenter the "free world." In short, opponents argue that these bans contribute significantly to the revolving door that now characterizes prisons.

Bans on social welfare programs vary from state to state. Our intent here is to paint a broad picture of the bans and we encourage the interested reader to visit the website of the Legal Action Center[5] and obtain their report for a more detailed understanding of the bans as they are imposed across the various states.

Cash Assistance and Food Stamps and Public Housing

Most states (thirty-eight) impose a ban on the receipt of cash assistance (TANF) and food stamps to individuals with a felony drug conviction. Nearly half of these states (seventeen) impose a *lifetime* ban on cash assistance and food stamps. The remaining twenty-one allow for the reinstatement of eligibility for these social welfare programs if certain conditions, such as successful treatment or a waiting period, have been met (Mukamal 2004). We underscore here the impact of these particular bans. Given the fact that individuals with a felony record face serious obstacles to employment—as we noted above (Pager 2003, 2007; Mukamal 2004) we ask the question, upon release from prison, struggling to find a job, facing a ban on cash assistance and food stamps, how will the reentry felon eat? Furthermore, as a result of specific changes in the drug laws that reclassified possession of five grams of crack-cocaine as a felony, the ban applies to those whose conviction is for a *possession*, and thus impacts millions of individuals whose real crime is an addiction, an issue we devote the entirety of chapter 3 to discussing. In contrast, *no similar ban is imposed on individuals with felony convictions that are not drug related.* The ban does not extend, for example, to those convicted of felony rape, murder, or child molestation. We wonder then about both the integrity of these bans but also their purpose especially in light of the fact that African Americans are disproportionately likely to be convicted of a drug felony (which carries the ban) whereas White men are disproportionately likely to be convicted of child molesting (which does not carry the ban).

The federal government also allows public housing authorities to use evidence of a criminal record in determining eligibility for public housing. The federal government imposes lifetime bans on eligibility for public housing on two groups: (1) those convicted of the production of methamphetamine and (2) those required to be registered for their lifetime on the state's sex offender registry. In addition, Mukamal's (2004) research of housing authority guidelines found that the majority of housing authorities *do consider* a person's criminal record when determining their eligibility for public housing. The most common bans were for felony drug convictions and violent offenses. Furthermore, her research noted that more than half, twenty-seven, of housing authorities "make decisions about eligibility for public housing based on *arrests that never led to a conviction*" (Mukamal 2004). Because children are most likely to live with their mothers, children of mothers with a drug felony will be ineligible to live in public housing. Therefore this ban poses a serious threat to the safe housing of more than one million African American children.

Student Loans

Recently, the system of higher education assistance that was available for inmates was dismantled by a key funding decision.

> The Higher Education Act of 1998 makes students convicted of drug-related offenses ineligible for any grant, loan, or work study assistance. This federal barrier cannot be lifted by states. *No other class of offense, including violent offenses, sex offenses, repeat offenses, or alcohol-related offenses, results in the automatic denial of federal financial aid eligibility.* (Mukamal 2004)

This single act completely dismantled the opportunities for inmates as well as reentry felons to pursue any post-secondary education. Research on wages, the racial and gender wage gaps, welfare to work, and recidivism all point to education as a key factor in eliminating inequality (Edin and Lein 1997; Mukamal 2004; Padavic and Reskin 2002). Higher education leads to better jobs, higher wages; it keeps people out of poverty, and it is closely tied to reducing recidivism. This ban, then, stands as yet another barrier to the successful reentry and reintegration of drug felons back into their families and communities.

Proponents of this law argue that it prevents drug users from using student loan monies to feed their drug habits. Opponents argue that it affects millions of incarcerated men and women and significantly reduces their possibilities for successful reentry. We wonder how many more times need we pose the question: what exactly is the desired outcome of this law? And, why does it target drug offenders and not violent offenders? Furthermore, because education is a key component to any rehabilitation program, this law seems to undermine any rehabilitation efforts that the system of "corrections" engages in.

Driver's License

Another outcome of the "reformation" of drug laws in the 1980s and 1990s was a law that allowed the federal government to deny highway funds to any state that refused to impose a minimum six-month revocation on the driver's license of individuals convicted of a felony drug offense (Mukamal 2004). And, though thirty-two states have modified this law to offer "restrictive licenses" that allow drug felons to travel to work, school, or treatment programs, eighteen states do not. Four states require that the revocation of the license last beyond 6 months (Mukamal 2004). Clearly driving restrictions significantly impact a reentry felon's chances of getting and holding a job. In fact the literature on welfare notes that one of the keys to a successful transition from welfare to work is having reliable transportation (Edin and Lein 1997).

Clearly the same applies to successful reentry. Thus, this driving restriction is one more barrier facing drug felons who are looking to turn their lives around. And, though many of the men we interviewed did not have the financial resources to purchase a vehicle, others noted that the lack of reliable public transportation, especially in the evening and on weekends, like the curfew at the homeless shelter, posed a significant barrier to their ability to hold and keep the kinds of jobs they were eligible for. Linwood, a sixty-something-year-old African American man who was recently released from prison after serving nearly twenty years, enthusiastically talked about the job he has working in the kitchen at a local restaurant: K&W.

After having cooked for many years in the cafeterias of several federal prisons, Linwood was thrilled at his good fortune: landing a job cooking at K&W while he watched so many other reentry felons struggle.[6] What troubles Linwood is the fact that he lives in a halfway house in the downtown part of town and the K&W where he works is more than ten miles away in the most outlying part of the northern "suburban" part of town. During the weekdays he can walk to the bus station and catch a bus—riding forty minutes or more—to his job. However, when he is assigned a shift that ends after 7 pm or on the weekends—which are the highest traffic times for restaurants and thus the shifts that are the most "full"—Linwood struggles to find coworkers who are willing to pick him up and/or take him home, especially because the halfway house where he lives is, as is typical, not near the most densely residential parts of the community. We wonder if Linwood and so many others like him will be able to sustain their employment despite barriers such as transportation. We know that their chance for successful reentry and thus the life chances of their families depends upon this success.

We conclude this section by asking what chance families, and disproportionately African American families, have of surviving the incarceration of one of their members, mothers and fathers, when they face such serious barriers to reentering the "free world" and reintegrating into family life. Reentry felons face barriers to employment, including bans on licensure, bans on the receipt of cash assistance and food stamps, disenfranchisement, driving restrictions, bans on public housing, and bans on obtaining funding for higher education. And, though these bans vary from state to state, the one constant theme is that all of the barriers and bans are the *most severe for drug felons*. And because a high percentage of African Americans are incarcerated for drug offenses *the impact on African American families is nothing short of devastating*.

What Happens When All Else Fails?

In our study we observed the development of prison-like communities in the "free world." We identified a core of individuals, mostly men, who cycle between prison and homeless shelters. They create a community inside prisons and then recreate it in the shelters and other locations where they spend time during the day and when they have exhausted their stay in a given shelter. We note that they differ from individuals who return from prison to a gang family, which provides a specific form of social capital that prevents members from falling into the trap of homelessness; this area of concern is beyond the scope of this book as interviews with key gang members and families is something we were unable to secure. Instead, we focus on these "prison communities on the outside," which contribute to a number of significant social problems, primarily those associated with the illegitimate economy (drugs, gambling, prostitution) but also robbery and assault (Ferman and Ferman 1973).

We will detail Nick's case in chapter 3, but a brief overview is relevant here. Nick spent nearly ten years in prison for felony drug convictions. Unlike many of the men and women we interviewed, Nick grew up in a middle-class family; he had privileges and advantages associated with financial stability and a supportive family. Nick graduated from college and worked for many years in the computer/IT industry in Washington, DC. At the height of his career, Nick was earning a six-figure salary, renting a condominium in an exclusive DC neighborhood, and was in all ways living the American Dream. For reasons Nick is unable to explain, or perhaps remember, he experimented with crack-cocaine. And, in his drug-induced words, he talked about how crack immediately took hold of his life; it grabbed him around the neck and never let go. In the period of a few short months Nick was fired, he was evicted from his condominium, his girlfriend left him, and he found himself a "crack-head" living on the street. Eventually Nick was arrested for possession of crack and he was sentenced to ten years in prison. After serving eight years, Nick was released from prison. Having lost everything, he found himself paroled to a homeless shelter. At the time we interviewed Nick, unable to beat his addiction[7] he had been cycling back and forth between homeless shelters and shorter stints in prison—primarily for "crimes" associated with homelessness—vagrancy, petty theft, and so forth. Nick's life makes clear that when reentry felons cannot find stable housing their fight to successfully rebuild their lives on the outside will be significantly more difficult.

Conclusion

With nearly 700,000 reentry felons returning to communities each year and more than 1,000 to Forsyth County, North Carolina, alone, where our data were collected, we can predict that unless this cycle of recidivism—the revolving prison door—is interrupted, it will not only continue but also grow, thus contributing to a rise in crime both locally and nationally. Furthermore, and of just as great a concern, in addition to recidivism, barriers to reentry—primarily homelessness and unemployment—put additional strain on social welfare agencies and charities that are already feeling an increasing burden brought on by the current recession, a burden that these agencies are not likely to be able to withstand. Additionally, because recidivism affects the family members of reentry felons—the majority of whom have minor children of whom they either have custody or child support obligations—their failures will continue to shackle their families and communities. In addition, the already-stretched social service agencies and charities who serve the families of the incarcerated—including the "welfare" system itself, food pantries, emergency clinics, and so forth—are likely to stretched beyond their capacities and the families of those who are incarcerated will fall further through the cracks. Thus, successful reentry is in the best interest of all of the public who pays taxes and provides philanthropic support to agencies like the United Way, the Salvation Army, and countless local organizations.

Success in Reentry

As we will detail in the book, there were some stories of success. Our interviews highlight the role that social networks can play in easing the transition out of prison, especially by providing access to housing and employment. In the next chapter we will discuss in detail the story of Lyman Sykes, an African American man in his mid-sixties who obtained his first job in the legitimate economy at the ripe age of sixty-two after having spent more than thirty-five years in prison. If we learn anything from Lyman's case it is that with the right kind of help and support, even an habitual felon, a former heroin addict, a man who spent more than half his life in prison, can get a job, keep the job, and move toward accessing the *American Dream*. Lyman's story provides an illustration of the ways in which recidivism can result in near-life sentences of the type Elsner (2006) and Haney and Zimbardo (1998) describe.

Notes

1. J. Petersilia Petersilia, (2000), "When Prisoners Return to the Community: Political, Economic, and Social Consequences," *Sentencing and Corrections: Issues for the 21st Century*, Washington, DC, U.S. Department of Justice Report notes that a disproportionate number of the incarcerated were unemployed or severely under-employed immediately before they were incarcerated.

2. Wright compares this to the genocide of the Native Americans during the colonial and revolutionary periods of U.S. history. He suggests that cordoning-off the under class in ghettos and prisons is considered morally superior to solutions like genocide, which are deemed morally abhorrent. It is important to note that Wright does not advocate this cordoning-off but rather is theorizing about a phenomenon he sees in the social world and the possibility that it is produced by the needs of capitalism.

3. We argue that prisons are an "ideal" location for cordoning-off because they constitute total institutions that can be completely designed and controlled to produce the desired effect. In contrast, rural and urban ghettos are organic and evolving places in which it is impossible for an institution or a government to have total control or produce outcomes that are desirable.

4. We address, later, the destruction that has been heaped on drug users especially by the set of laws known under the rubric simply as the "Rockefeller Drug Laws." Taken together, these have drastically increased the prison populations nationwide.

5. Legal Action Center, www.lac.org.

6. We will return to Linwood's case in chapter 6 as his, like Lyman Syke's, illustrates the role of social capital in securing employment.

7. Like most inmates, Nick did not receive any drug treatment in prison.

3

The Role of Addiction

If there's a bright side to a financial emergency, it's the opportunity a crisis brings to stop spending money on things that aren't working. . . . There are alternatives. . . . Put aside the fact that substance abuse treatment saves the lives of people plagued by chronic addiction. The savings to taxpayers ought to be enough to force a reconsideration of policies that haven't worked: It costs $48,000 a year to keep an addict in prison, compared to $4,000 to $5,000 for outpatient treatment. (Metrowest Daily News 2009)

THERE IS A STRONG RELATIONSHIP BETWEEN DRUG USE and incarceration. This relationship is important for a variety of reasons, including the role that it plays in filling prison cells, the racial disparities that are a direct result of differential treatment of various substances, and the development of policies that shape both drug sentences and also social welfare programs. At the individual level, the men we interviewed told stories of tragedy, multidecade addiction, disrupted family life, and the constant struggle for survival. In this chapter we will provide a context for understanding the relationship between drug use and the criminal justice system and use this context to analyze the experiences of those men whose lives we studied. We begin with a review of the relevant statistics regarding drug use and then examine the critical changes in drug policy that occurred during the latter part of the twentieth century.

Drug Use

Across the twentieth century American's attitudes around drugs (and alcohol) have changed in terms of both drug and alcohol use as well as in terms of the use of the criminal justice system to regulate drugs and alcohol. One common misperception is that the dramatic rise in arrests, convictions, and incarceration for drug charges reflects an overall increase in the number and percent of Americans who are using controlled substances. In fact, research by the White House Office of National Drug Control Policy (ONDCP) Information Clearinghouse,[1] which has collected data on drug use, categorized by age, beginning in 1975 to the present, shows overwhelmingly, in every category, that drug use rose from 1975 to 1979 and then dropped of significantly in the 1980s, 1990s and early 2000s. These declines occurred in every age group and for every period for which data were collected. For example, the percent of Americans over the age of 12 who reported using an "illicit substance" in the last thirty days declined from 14 percent in 1975 to 7 percent in 2002. Similarly, the percent of Americans who reported they had ever used an illicit substance dropped from 32 percent in 1975 to 28 percent in 2002. Thus, the evidence is overwhelmingly clear that the three-fold increase in drug convictions between 1980 and 2008 are not in response to increased drug use, but rather to changes in the criminalization of substances (which occurred slowly across the entire twentieth century) and changes in the policies designed to address drug possession.

Drug Policies

In response to the trends and overall increased criminalization of drugs across the twentieth century lawmakers felt there was a need to make significant changes to the way in which drug possession (and dealing) was handled in the criminal justice system. The logic was that the "War on Drugs," as President Ronald Reagan termed it, could be fought in part through deterrence: if sentences for drug possession were harsh enough, people would stop using drugs. Thus were born the Rockefeller Drug Laws.

In summary, the "War on Drugs" officially began in 1972 with a formal announcement by President Richard Nixon. The "War on Drugs" officially heated up under the administration of President Ronald Reagan, who added the position of "Drug Czar" to the President's Executive Office. The "War on Drugs" did not so much criminalize substances, as that had been happening across the early part of the twentieth century. What it did do was put into place stiffer sentencing guidelines that required (1) longer sentences; (2) mandatory minimums; (3) some drug offenses to be moved from the misdemeanor category to the felony category; and (4) the institution of the "Three Strikes You're Out" policy (Mauer 2001; Roberts 2004).

- Longer sentences: Today most of the defendants convicted of crack-cocaine possession receive an average sentence of eleven years (King and Mauer 2006).
- Mandatory minimums: The most frequently cited example is the sentencing guidelines for possession of crack-cocaine. As part of the "War on Drugs," a conviction of possessing five grams of crack now mandates a five-year minimum sentence (Meierhoefer 1992).
- Felonizing drug offenses: Small possession convictions, particularly of crack-cocaine, were recategorized from misdemeanors to felonies in the 1986 Drug Abuse Act (King and Mauer 2006).
- "Three Strikes You're Out": This law allows for life sentences for convicts receiving a third felony conviction. Coupled with the recategorizing of some drug possession offenses (i.e., crack cocaine) as felonies, the result has been that many inmates serving life sentences have been convicted of nothing more than three drug possession offenses; in effect, they are serving life sentences for untreated addiction (Haney and Zimbardo 1998).

One of the clearest outcomes of these changes in drug sentencing is the rapid increase in the number of inmates. According to the agency of the federal government that is charged with keeping all of the state and federal statistics on crime—the Bureau of Justice Statistics—between 1996 and 2002 drug convictions increased 37 percent and represent the largest source of the growth in prison populations during this time period.[3] Along with the increase in the number of inmates has been the rise in the number of prisons built to house them.[4]

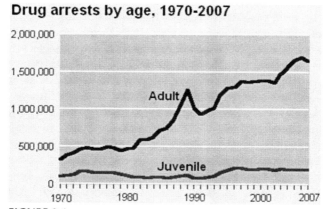

FIGURE 3.1
Growth in drug arrests 1970–2007

In order to contextualize the situation in the United States let's examine incarceration rates internationally. The United States has the highest incarceration rate in the world, greater than countries we often associate with high rates of incarceration including Russia, China, and Iran (recall figure 1.2 in chapter 1).

Specifically with regards to drug convictions, currently 450,000 of the more than two million inmates (45 percent) in U.S. state and federal prison are incarcerated for nonviolent drug offenses. In contrast, this is more people than the European Union, an entity with 100 million more people than the United States, has in prison for *all crimes combined*. Individual states and the federal government continue to spend about $10 billion a year imprisoning drug offenders, and billions more on the "War on Drugs." And these costs do not include the impact incarceration has on the economic and social life of the country, individual states, and communities. When we consider the role that race plays in drug convictions, we note that because inmates incarcerated for nonviolent drug offenses are disproportionately likely to be African American the impact on the African American community is devastating (Roberts 2004). What this means is that young men (and increasingly women)[5] have a higher chance of landing in jail, at some point in their adult years, more so than ever before.

Crack-Cocaine

One of the most important and decisive changes to the drug policies that began being implemented in the 1980s revolved around drawing distinctions between two forms of cocaine: crack (or rock) and powder. Crack is created by cooking powder cocaine with baking soda; the residual or "rocks" are what we commonly refer to as crack. It is commonly believed that crack was developed as a way to deliver a similar high in a cheaper form. Because crack is less pure than cocaine its street value is significantly lower. Many of the men and women we interviewed talked about buying or selling a "rock" for around $20. As a result, the crack epidemic of the 1980s and early 1990s exploded largely as a result of the heavy marketing of crack in low-income communities, much as "meth" is today, and as a result, by the early 1980s, around the same time that the Rockefeller Drug Laws were being developed, crack had become associated with black urban ghettos and with it the image of the "crack head" was an African American man or woman. In contrast, the more expensive powder cocaine was largely associated with the upper-class professional community as well as with Hollywood. Readers may remember that by the late 1980s it was common to see the latest victim of a cocaine binge—often a child movie star like Dana Plato, who starred in the television hit show "Different Strokes"—in handcuffs or a mug shot displayed on the nightly news.[6] Many who study drug policy argue that as a result of racialized differential use of crack versus cocaine, drug policies regarding crack and cocaine developed in a racialized manner as well.

In sum, federal drug policy draws a distinction between crack and powder cocaine and sets a one-hundred-to-one sentencing disparity between the two forms. This means that distribution of just five grams of crack-cocaine (about a thimble full) yields a five-year mandatory minimum sentence, while it takes 500 grams of powder cocaine to trigger the same five-year sentence. Crack-cocaine is the only drug for which there is a federal mandatory minimum sentence for mere possession. Proponents of this ratio in sentencing argue that it is simple chemistry. Because it takes one-hundred grams of cocaine (powder) to make one gram of crack (rock), sentences ought to reflect differences in the amount of "high" that is derived from different amounts of cocaine when it is consumed in different forms—thus the 100:1 ratio that is employed in the sentencing guidelines.[7] We note here that this would be equivalent to tying alcohol possession laws—for minors, in violation of open-container laws and so forth—to the "proof" of the alcohol that is possessed such that illegal possession of "three-two" beer (beer that is no more than 3.2 percent alcohol) would carry a lighter sentence than the illegal possession of eighty-proof vodka. Laws governing the possession of alcohol have never been applied differently with regards to the percent of alcohol in the beverage and most Americans would probably find the idea preposterous. Similarly, the laws around the illegal possession of narcotic prescription drugs do not vary based on the number of milligrams of the drug per tablet. Yet, this is just what the crack-cocaine laws do.

A second issue is the fact that the new drug policies treat crack differently than other banned substances, including powder cocaine. Simple possession of any quantity of any other substance by a first-time offender—including powder cocaine—is a misdemeanor offense punishable by a maximum of one year in prison. (21 U.S.C. 844). In contrast, simple possession of crack, by a first time offender, is a class C felony, carrying a mandatory five-year minimum sentence and the offender carries a felony conviction on his or her record.

This sentencing disparity, enacted in 1986 at the height of drug war, was based largely on the myth that crack-cocaine was more dangerous than powder cocaine and that it was instantly addictive and caused violent behavior. Since then, copious amounts of scientific evidence and an analysis by the U.S. Sentencing Commission have shown that these assertions were not supported by sound data and were exaggerated or outright false.

The crack/powder disparity also fuels racial disparities. In 2006, 82 percent of those sentenced under federal crack-cocaine laws were Black, and only 8.8 percent were White—even though more than two-thirds of people who use crack-cocaine are White (2007). The U.S. Sentencing Commission has found that "sentences appear to be harsher and more severe for racial minorities than others as a result of this law. The current penalty structure results in a perception of unfairness and inconsistency" (2007).

In response to these critiques, two reforms in late 2007 built momentum for reforming this unfair disparity. First, the U.S. Supreme Court ruled, in *United States v. Kimbrough*, that judges have the authority to sentence individuals below the recommended federal sentencing guideline recommendation in crack-cocaine cases. Second, the U.S. Sentencing Commission proffered an amendment, which was unopposed by Congress and went into effect on November 1, 2007, to lower guideline sentence recommendations by two levels, saving defendants approximately sixteen months of prison time. The USSC then voted to make this amendment reducing recommended sentences for crack-cocaine offenses retroactive, saving individuals, on average, twenty-seven months of prison-time. The practical effect of that vote may, pending a judicial review in each case, impact the sentences of up to 19,500 currently incarcerated individuals who may, as a result of these reforms, be eligible for early release over the next three decades. Congress is now considering a number of bills that would partially or completely reform the disparity. To the reader unfamiliar with either drug sentencing or the impact of felonies on reentry, we point out that this type of change in policy would not only reduce the long sentences that many inmates are currently serving for simple possession offenses, but if in addition, first-time offenders possessing small amounts of crack were charged with misdemeanors instead of felonies, this would dramatically ease the reentry process for these ex-offenders, primarily because job applications require the disclosure of a felony conviction but not of a misdemeanor possession, which is a significant barrier to employment, as noted in chapter 2.

Perhaps one of the greatest barriers to successful reentry for those individuals with a drug felony conviction is the series of bans on social welfare. As noted in chapter 2, the vast majority of so-called safety net programs that fall under the rubric "social welfare" have restrictions and in some cases lifetime bans for those convicted of a felony. Of particular importance to our discussion here is the special "attention" that the legislative authors of these bans placed on drug felons. The reader will recall, for example, that only two groups face a lifetime ban on access to public housing—child molesters and those with a drug felony conviction—and only one group faces a lifetime ban on cash assistance, food stamps, and access to federal student loans: drug felons. As noted, as a result of the changing drug laws these bans on housing, cash assistance, food stamps, and educational assistance apply in many cases to individuals who have been convicted on a *single possession charge*. As a result, as our case studies will illustrate, in addition to fighting their often-untreated addictions, drug felons face perhaps the steepest road to successful reentry of all individuals released from prison.

Losing Everything: Crack and Powder Cocaine

As important as the statistics on drug and alcohol use and abuse are, it is the stories of the individual men and women we interviewed that are the most compelling part to the saga. Of the twenty-five individuals we interviewed for this project, only one had never been incarcerated in jail or prison on drug charges. Thus, it is clear that at least among the men and women that we identified through their involvement in a reentry program, they were overwhelmingly likely to have been incarcerated on drug convictions and, secondly, they were frequently continuing to battle an addiction. And, though our sample is unique in that it is comprised of people seeking help with their reentry, we argue that it is otherwise typical; the seeming over-representation of drug felons is in fact consistent with the national data on drug convictions—a quarter of all inmates in state prison were convicted of a drug-related crime (Rosenmerkel, Durose et al. 2009). Additionally, the stories of the men and women we interviewed illustrate the role that addiction plays as a barrier to successful reentry and this is unlikely to vary across any population of drug felons. Lastly, as is extremely common among incarcerated populations, several of the men and women we interviewed were incarcerated primarily for another crime—as are the cases of Eddie and Brandon, two sex offenders we interviewed whose stories we tell in chapter 4. Both men served time, typically in jail, separate from their prison terms, on possession charges, usually for marijuana, and they served additional time on top of the primary sex-related charge for possession of drugs. Here we tell the stories of a few of the men we interviewed whose stories are the most compelling and illustrate most graphically the role that drug and alcohol addiction play in the cycle of incarceration and reentry.

Nick[8]

When we interviewed him, Nick was a thirty-something African American man who looked at least twenty years older than he was. At the time of the interview, Nick was living in the homeless shelter, though he reported that he had been chronically homeless for the last several years. Nick served ten years in state prison for the possession of crack-cocaine, and had been out for a couple of years by the time we interviewed him. Though Nick had not been re-arrested since his release, it was clear that his addiction was not under control. He admitted that he was still using crack and that his homelessness and his disheveled appearance were a direct result of his addiction.

Nick's case best illustrates the tragedy of losing everything due to an addiction. Nick was raised in a middle-class family near Charlotte, North Carolina. Though Nick grew up in a single-parent home, his mother earned a good living and his grandparents played a significant role in helping to raise him. Like many young men, Nick didn't work as hard as he should have during middle and high school, but other than a few skirmishes, Nick stayed out of trouble, graduated from high school, and did well enough to be admitted to college. In college, Nick studied computer science and after completing a two-year degree at a local community college, Nick found a job in the Charlotte area working as a computer technologist. It was obvious during the interview that Nick was extremely proud of this part of his life. He almost glowed while talking about his career. He advanced quickly at work and after a relatively short period of time he was offered a promotion and a transfer to work in the Washington, DC, area. Despite being a self-described "home body," Nick took the job and relocated.

It was very obvious that this was a time in Nick's life when he felt happy and in control. He was working, he had rented a beautiful condo in the DC area, he had money, and over time he had a series of intimate relationships. In a span of nine months or so Nick would lose all of this to his addiction to crack.

One weekend, Nick was hanging out with some friends from work and one of the folks at the party pulled out some crack and offered Nick an opportunity to try it. Nick smoked crack for the first time that night and he woke the next day wanting to smoke again. After just one weekend, Nick was hooked. He described the addiction, which happened very quickly, in this way: "It was like crack grabbed me around the throat and never let go."

The research on crack and cocaine addictions suggests that the addict prefers using the drug to all other activities and will use the drug until the user or the supply is exhausted. Addicts will exhibit behavior entirely different from their previous lifestyle, including leading them to perform unusual acts compared with their former standards of conduct. For example, a cocaine user may sell her child to obtain more cocaine. There are many stories of professionals, such as lawyers, physicians, bankers, and athletes, with daily habits costing hundreds to thousands of dollars, with binges in the $20,000–$50,000 range.[9] The result may be loss of job and profession, loss of family, bankruptcy, and death. And, this was clearly the case for Nick.

For several months Nick was able to hide his addiction because he used mostly alone and at home. But, within nine months of his initial use, Nick's addiction had spiraled out of control. His habit was costing more per day than he was earning and so he began falling behind on his rent and other monthly bills in order to "free up" the cash he needed to get the next "fix." Nick and his girlfriend, who he said he had intended to marry, began fighting over his use of crack. Eventually, unable to go to work regularly because he was always high, Nick lost his job. Shortly after that, already behind on his rent, he was evicted. Controlled by his addiction, Nick would buy crack on "credit," and now homeless and using in public places, and unable to pay back his suppliers, Nick was eventually arrested as part of a "sting" operation in DC. Nick pled guilty to possession of crack and, based on mandatory minimum sentencing guidelines, he was sentenced to ten years in state prison (he served his time in Maryland). He served eight and a half years and was released back into the free world about two years before we interviewed him.

A common misconception is that prison is a reasonable approach to treating drug addiction. Why? Perhaps it can be conceptualized as a combination of "in-patient" treatment—the inmate is forcibly incarcerated—and required withdrawal. Certainly the prison environment involves the containment of individuals. Though, we would argue that forcibly detaining an individual as an approach to drug treatment runs counter to the advice of many experts who argue that especially in an in-patient setting, an individual is far more likely to successfully kick the habit if she or he *consents* to the treatment. In this way, prisons are not at all like in-patient drug treatment programs. Secondly, it is a huge myth that prison confinement removes an individual's access to drugs. Every ex-offender we have ever talked to, including exonerees, one of whose story we will tell in chapter 7, put it this way: "Anything you have on the outside you have on the inside." This holds true for access to sex, drugs, and virtually everything else. In fact, one of our interviewees, Llee, claimed that as a long-term inmate he rose through the ranks to the point that he was overseeing the system of bringing drugs into the prison in which he was incarcerated and managing their distribution. He also claims to have developed a romantic relationship with a female guard and that they routinely had sexual intercourse during his incarceration. And, Lyman, whose case we will discuss later in this chapter, indicated that in fact he was *first introduced to drugs inside prison.* Thus, incarceration, at least for the drug addict, can only be described as punishment; *it is not treatment.*

After serving eight and a half years in prison, Nick was released in to the "free world" as addicted to crack as he had been the day he was sentenced. Yet, now he found himself without any financial support and no place to live. This is another extremely common experience for drug addicts who are often released from prison only to find themselves unemployable and homeless. Nick found his way to the drug-addicted homeless community in DC and was able to feed his habit by stealing, selling a few drugs on the street—he never aspired to nor did he become a big dealer or major player like Llee did—and trading whatever he could for crack. Across this time he would create relationships with women, often women who offered to help him, only to see these relationships bring him nothing but trouble. In one case he was in a relationship with a woman who was also a crack addict. She was living with her boyfriend, a non-addict, and she convinced Nick that together she and Nick could rob the apartment she shared with him, sell the property they stole, and buy more crack. Nick agreed to her plan and found himself arrested for breaking and entering. It seems his "girlfriend" had not broken things off with the man with whom she lived and he called the police when he found Nick and the woman together in his apartment. These types of things continued to occur and Nick did short stints in county jails as a result.

Eventually Nick moved back to North Carolina hoping that he would find some support from his family. He did move back in with his mother and grandmother for a short period of time, but they were unwilling to put up with his addiction and all of its attendant consequences and they threw him out. As a result, Nick has been cycling among the homeless shelters in Winston-Salem for more than a year.

The Cycle of Homelessness

Like most cities of its size, Winston-Salem has several different types of homeless shelters—in addition to the battered women's shelter—that provide services to homeless men. Each shelter has different rules and requirements, though what they share in common is a limit on the number of consecutive nights that an individual can spend before they must leave, with most shelters having limits of sixty to ninety days. As a result, Nick has cycled among the shelters that offer housing for men. And, he shared that he has spent several additional months living in the kudzu covered "community" that some of chronically homeless in Winston-Salem have created. It is not only within a block of several shelters for both men and women, but it is also a "hot spot" for drug addicts. Among the homeless, 38 percent report alcohol use problems and 26 percent report other drug use problems.[10]

By the end of the two-hour interview, Nick was visibly agitated. He was sweating profusely and had begun to fidget almost uncontrollably. As we handed Nick the $50 he received as a gesture to thank him for participating in the interview we knew he would be headed down to the kudzu village to buy another rock of crack. It was disheartening to watch a thirty-something-year-old man who looked like he was fifty, with dirty clothes, dirty hair, whose teeth were brown and nails were filthy, walk back out into a world he had once had a place in. His college education a long-forgotten credential, unable to kick his addiction to crack, with the label "ex-felon," unemployed and cycling between homeless shelters, Nick lives so far out on the margins that the likelihood he will ever reenter the mainstream world of renting an apartment, shopping for healthy food at the local grocery, or buying a new outfit or pair of shoes at the mall seems remote.

"The Key to Dealing Is Never to Use": William and Llee

In many ways, William's story is similar in its tragedy. Born into an intact, middle-class family, William's parents separated and divorced when he was three years old. The break-up forced his mother to move into public housing while his father and his new wife lived a solid middle-class lifestyle in Charleston, South Carolina.

William had a difficult time moving between the two worlds his parents created and, as the oldest child, he felt a great deal of responsibility for his younger siblings. This was exacerbated by the fact that his siblings were half-siblings who had different fathers from his own. Unlike his own father, who provided him with all of the kinds of resources and opportunities that middle-class parents can provide, his siblings were afforded nothing like this from their own fathers. William's responsibility was compounded when he was sixteen and his mother, a drug addict and prostitute, ran away to Tennessee, leaving him and his younger siblings with their eighty-year-old grandmother. As much as William would have benefited from living with his father, who not only had the financial resources to provide opportunities for William but who also ran a "tight ship" as William described it, he felt guilty and responsible for his younger siblings.

Falling into the wrong crowd, William was incarcerated for the first time shortly after his mother abandoned them. He was sixteen years old. William and some of his friends decided that they needed a car but they didn't have any money. So, they started hot wiring cars for joy riding. This activity quickly progressed to stealing cars off of used car lots and they were eventually caught when they brashly drove stolen cars to school. William spent eighteen months in a youth detention facility and shortly after being released "changed up my whole scenario. I started selling drugs." William rationalizes that he sold drugs because he couldn't make enough money in the legitimate economy, working minimum wage jobs, to support himself and help his younger siblings. William is distinct, compared to many of the other people we interviewed who were selling drugs; (1) he never used the drugs he was selling and (2) he always maintained a regular job in the legitimate economy alongside his drug dealing. The issue of using drugs while one is simultaneously selling drugs is interesting. The more "successful" former drug dealers whom we interviewed insisted that they did not use drugs. The rationale was simple: if you used up your own product you went home empty-handed. Ironically, for many of the former dealers we interviewed, several of whom spent more than a decade in prison, their downfall came after they did start to use and the addiction took over.

In addition to abiding by the "no using" principle, William also credits his maintenance of a legitimate job for keeping him from getting into worse trouble. Analytically what makes sense about this is that compared to Nick, by keeping one foot in the legitimate economy William was keeping at least one foot in the mainstream. It is likely that this toehold in part prevented him from moving farther and farther out in to the margins.

William was a late teenager when he first began to get arrested for drugs. This was in the mid-1990s before the most severe sentencing guidelines went in to effect. As a result, like many of the other men we interviewed, William's first sentences were relatively short: in his first stint he did only three and a half years on a ten-year cocaine conviction. But, once released, William made a habit of violating his parole—sometimes by getting arrested for selling drugs and other times for incidents as minor as failing to report to his parole officer (P.O.)—and as a result, he was continuously having suspended time on his sentences reactivated.

Perhaps because of his regular stints in the county jail or short stays in state prisons, or perhaps because of his entrepreneurial spirit, by age twenty-five William had become embedded into one of the biggest drug rings in the county. He was making enough money selling drugs to pay the rent on several apartments—one for his sister, one for his aunt, and one for him—and to provide all the other support they needed to live. Tired of paying his younger brother's bills,[11] he recruited him into selling drugs as well. They were moving several kilos of cocaine—with a street value of approximately $50,000—per week.

Early one morning in July of 2004 William received a call on his cell phone from a man who wanted to buy some marijuana. After the transaction took place the man William had sold the drugs to accused William of not giving him the amount he had paid for. He shot William in the lower back. The bullet ripped through William's lower abdomen leaving him severely injured and with a lifelong reminder: a colostomy.

Frustrated that the man who shot him received only eighteen months in prison, William complained to the police department and in this interaction he learned volumes about the attitudes many people—the police and the general public—have about ex-convicts:

> "We already know that ya'll are violent criminals, ya'll are convicted criminals, and if ya'll do anything else we're going to give you 11 to 14 years and the state will pay it." That stopped me. But then right after that, couldn't find a job or anything, so I went right back to selling drugs.

On and off throughout his life William, like many of the other men we interviewed, had intimate relationships and sometimes these relationships resulted in children. William has two children, a son who was born while he was in prison, and a daughter. Though William does not have custody of his daughter, he does have a relationship with her that amounts to far more than the child support payments he is legally bound to make.

Though William was one of the most intelligent men we interviewed, he continued to make bad choices in his life. About a year before we interviewed him, William had an argument with his common-law wife. The argument grew violent and both William and his wife grabbed weapons. William's wife shot him in the foot. Engaging in chivalry and wanting to protect her, when the police arrived William claimed the injury was self-inflicted. What William had failed to consider is the fact that as a convicted felon he is not allowed to possess a firearm. He was arrested and charged with "felony possession of a firearm." Coupled with a warrant for not paying child support, he served five more months in prison.

At the time of the interview, William had been out of prison for several months. Unlike every other release, this time he walked across the street from the courthouse to the reentry project with whom we partner. When we asked William what was different this time he responded:

> Man, I'm 35 years old and I don't have anything to show and prove that I'm 35 years old. That was really depressing because when I got shot, I wasn't scared of dying. The fear of death didn't kick in. I felt a feeling of disappointment.

Despite his record of nearly twenty years in and out of prison, with the help of the reentry program and the "vouching" of the voice of the project, Darryl Hunt, William was able to get a job washing dishes in a local restaurant. The last time we checked in on William he was still working and it appears that he has finally gotten his life together. What is different about William than about the countless other men we interviewed who served similar time and who had a list of felony drug convictions a mile long? As we suggest above, William was selling drugs but he wasn't using drugs. Unlike Nick, who "invests" every dollar he can get into another rock of crack, William is not shackled by an untreated addiction. Secondly, William has always had one foot anchored in the legitimate economy. This experiences with getting a job, handling a time card, paying taxes, and cashing a paycheck provide a sort of cultural capital that allows William, even after a relatively long five-year sentence in prison, to slide right back into the legitimate work economy, though he often "slid back in to dealing drugs" as well. And, compared to so many others, William's exposure to a middle-class lifestyle seems to have stuck with him. His aspirations to make something of himself coupled with his work experience and his lack of addiction may be the right nexus so that William can "make it" this time and end his cycle of selling drugs and serving prison terms.

When we interviewed Llee he was in his early thirties and had just been released from serving fifteen years in prison for selling crack. Llee arrived at the interview well dressed, bedecked in gold jewelry and wearing sunglasses, which he did not remove once during the interview. He was indeed "blinged out." Llee is in many ways typical of many of the African American men we interviewed, even taking into consideration all of the "fish tales" we were told, by all accounts he was the most successful drug dealer we met. Like so many other African American men we interviewed, Llee grew up in the housing projects of Winston-Salem, North Carolina. Growing up in a neighborhood with very little economic opportunity and very few examples of men, in particular, going off to work each day (Wilson 1996), Llee gravitated toward the older boys in his community who had money: the drug dealers. Llee enjoyed being a "player" and he quickly rose through the ranks of the drug operation in his neighborhood. As a result, he was given permission to deal drugs in a wider geographic area, including at a local middle and high school, which allowed him to increase his contacts and earn significantly more money. By the time Llee was arrested—as part of a sting operation designed to bring down mid-level players like Llee—he was supervising younger dealers who worked for him, had a house full of weapons, drove a nice car, was well dressed, and had a roll of cash that made him both a player and vulnerable.

Llee was vulnerable to both other dealers and gang members who wanted to "negotiate" for his distribution region and to lower-level dealers who could be convinced to snitch on him when they were arrested, thus reducing their own sentences. This is exactly what happened. According to Llee, the police instigated a sting that was actually designed to bring down higher-level drug dealers who were transporting drugs into North Carolina from the Texas-Mexico border. As part of the sting, Llee and some dealers who were higher in the hierarchy than him were arrested. Tens of thousands of dollars of drugs were confiscated and heavy prison sentences were sent down, including fifteen years for Llee. Unlike Nick or William, who had served relatively short sentences and struggled to successfully reenter the "free world," Llee had spent his entire adult life incarcerated and his story of reentry was still to be written. What we learned about Llee included a detailed account of his experience moving up the ladder in the world of the illegitimate economy of the drug trade and he confirmed what others had already said, that every conceivable product and service that we are accustomed to in the "free world" can be obtained on the inside.

Llee approached prison much as he had approached drug dealing; since he knew he was going to have to spend a good number of years locked up he decided to use his time wisely and he aspired to move up through the prison hierarchy. He did just that. By his account, Llee was a major player in the distribution of contraband that was moving in and out of the prison. He claims to have wooed a female guard, he referred to her as his "girlfriend," through whom he could move contraband, including drugs and pornography, but also, on occasion, cell phones, or at least access to using a cell phone to make a call to the "free world." Of course he collected a "fee" for brokering these transactions, which he extracted from other inmates, though he assured us that his "sexual services" were all that was required of him to compensate the guard for carrying the contraband in from the "free world." Interestingly Llee recounted that on the day of his release his "girlfriend," who was working in a different prison from the one he was released from, refused to be part of his homecoming party, claiming instead that she had to work. He felt so slighted by her, for he had expected that once he was released they would live together and pursue a relationship under more "normal" circumstances, that he responded by hooking up with another woman—a White woman—who his friends invited to the homecoming party.

Of course stories such as those told by Llee must be taken with a grain of salt, much like the fishing tales that fathers and husbands tell when they return from a week at fish camp, but certainly most of what Llee reports is basically true; it is just exaggerated. Like many drug dealers (Venkatesh 2008), for all the "glory" and power Llee had as a player in the drug ring in Winston-Salem, upon his release, with nowhere else to go, Llee found himself living, as a thirty-something-year-old man, with his mother. When we interviewed Llee he was still living with his mother. And, as "payment" she required him to do things like mow the lawn. It was clear in the interview that Llee felt that mowing the lawn was a task that was beneath him—a man who at the height of his career could deliver just about anything—but with no one else willing to help him in his time of need, he was obligated to keep his mother happy so that he could keep a roof over his head and food in his stomach.

As we noted, at the time of the interview it was difficult to predict the pathway Llee's reentry will take. That said, like William, he has a couple of things going for him. First, he is not a drug addict. He was selling thousands of dollars of crack per week, but he was not using his product. This is one obstacle he will not have to overcome. Second, we suggest that if he can harness the skills that he used to become a successful player in the drug trade on the outside and as a "king pin" in the operation of the importing of contraband while in prison, Llee may be able to transform these skills and his experience into the legitimate economy. But, as both William and Lyman's stories confirm, he will have to modify his expectations so that he is satisfied working for relatively low wages and implementing a savings plan rather than relying on "fast money" to obtain the material status markers he deeply desires.

Where Is the Hope? Kicking the Addiction: Lyman

The case of Lyman Sykes is so compelling that we will return to it on many occasions throughout the chapters in this book. Lyman, whose nickname is the "Shoe Man," is an African American man we interviewed when he was in his early sixties. At the time of the interview, Lyman had been back in the "free world" for eighteen months or so, the longest stint ever since he was first sent to a juvenile detention center when he was a young teenager perhaps fifty years ago. Lyman can't tell you how long he has been in prison, because most of his sentences have been under ten years. What he can tell you is that he has spent somewhere close to thirty-five years in prison and that the Christmas before we interviewed him was the first he could remember celebrating in the "free world." Lyman's case will illustrate specific points germane to our discussion of the importance of social capital to successful reentry (chapter 6). Here we analyze Lyman's case in order to illustrate some of the key issues that are relevant to our discussion of drug addiction and the experience of reentry.

Lyman began his criminal career as a petty thief. As a young teenager in the late 1950s Lyman found himself, much like William, with a great deal of responsibility for himself and his siblings. Lyman's father was in prison—for attempting to murder his mother—and his mother, bound to a wheelchair as a result of the injuries she sustained at the hands of his father—died. Lyman admits that he always had a penchant for "shiny" things, including shoes, which is where he got his nickname, and beginning before his mother died, he would earn money legitimately—by shining the shoes of soldiers who were stationed in nearby Virginia Beach—but when this wasn't generating enough income to buy what he desired, Lyman began stealing. "I really wanted to be a player, a pimp."

The first thing he stole, at age twelve, was a bike. He had desperately wanted a bike for Christmas, but his mother, disabled and wheelchair bound, was entirely dependent on welfare and on the kindness of others. Though there were gifts under the Christmas tree and a ham on the dinner table, Lyman was determined to fill his desire for a bike on his own, so he stole one. By the time he was fourteen he was stealing cars . . . mostly to joy ride around town. These activities led to Lyman being sent on many occasions for short stints in juvenile detention. Interestingly, Lyman was an excellent athlete and it was not uncommon for the high school coach to get Lyman temporarily released from detention upon promising he would return him after the game. Though Lyman admits that he spent "most of his teenage years in reform school" he played in enough basketball games to be offered a scholarship to play at Howard University. For a young man growing up in the segregated south, this would be the opportunity of a lifetime.

> I scored 35 points in a basketball game on a Wednesday and on a Thursday I was in a jail reading about it. Just before Christmas. The police came into school and carried me, boots, desk, and all to jail.

By the time he was eighteen, Lyman was sentenced to the Virginia Department of Corrections and "admitted" to the penitentiary. Lyman did so many discreet sentences in the penitentiary that it was difficult for him to recall which arrests and convictions occurred when and what sentences they resulted in. Basically, from age nineteen to age thirty-one or thirty-two Lyman's primary crimes were theft, breaking and entering and other property crimes. He spent the majority of his twenties in prison, though he remarked that every time he got out he managed to "improve the population" by fathering a couple of children. He has a total of nine children with at least four different women.

Unlike the other cases we have profiled in this chapter, Lyman didn't begin using drugs until he was in his early thirties. Lyman was adamant: "I never wanted to become a drug addict. That was the farthest thing from my mind." But, during a period of incarceration, several tragedies occurred to his loved ones in the "free world" and unable to help, because he was locked up, Lyman sought solace in drugs. He was first introduced to an inmate concoction that involved cooking up Tylenol and Benadryl much like one might cook up crack out of cocaine. This mixture is then injected and it has an effect similar to that of heroin. Lyman was hooked. Back on the outside, in the late 1960s and early 1970s the drug culture had rapidly expanded. In Lyman's case this was not so much a function of the so-called hippie generation that experimented with marijuana and hallucinogens like LSD, for this was not Lyman's culture. Rather, Lyman fell into the heroin culture that developed largely around Vietnam vets, both African American and White, who returned addicted to heroin. Lyman found a market for his talents—we can assure the reader that having interviewed and interacted with Lyman repeatedly over the last few years that he has a persuasive and charismatic personality such that he could sell ice to an Eskimo—and he found a way to feed the addiction that now shackled him.

Lyman's introduction to heroin and his involvement in the drug trade roughly correspond to the height of the drug reform laws. As a result, Lyman's sentences for possession and dealing drugs rapidly increased across the three decades (mid-1970s to mid-2000s) in which Lyman was heavily engaged in the drug culture, both as a user and as a dealer. Though we will focus on Lyman's experiences with reentry in chapter 6, it is important to point out here that Lyman credits his successful reentry to a number of forces, but at the core is the fact that he was able to kick the heroin habit. When we talked to Lyman about why he was able to get a job and keep it, as a sixty-two-year-old man with more than three decades of incarceration and a list of felonies so long it would fill a notebook, he demonstrated the problem of addiction: the heroin slump. Lyman slumped over, let his eyes glaze, and his mouth slack. He then returned to his normal posture and asked, with all seriousness, "who can work like that?"

His remark, "who can work like that," is part of the key to this discussion. Lyman's successful reentry, he has now been out of prison for more than three years, he has risen to the position of assistant manager at a local fast food restaurant, he owns his own car, he has reconciled with his wife—remarking that he never knew sex was so good till he had it sober!—he babysits his grandchildren, he ponders getting his GED, and on November 4, 2008, Lyman Sykes, aged sixty-two, voted for the first time in his life, is largely centered on his ability to break his addiction to heroin. Lyman was able to get access to the recommended treatment for heroin: methadone. And, when we interviewed him in June 2008 he was pleased to note that he had been clean for "five years last January" and he credits his soberness for his ability to rebuild his life.

Clearly Lyman had many other things going for him, including a wife who was willing to take him back and the friendship and support of the founder of the reentry program, Mr. Darryl Hunt, but as the other cases profiled in this chapter have demonstrated clearly, without treatment there is little hope that men (or women) with drug felony convictions will be able to successfully reenter the "free world" and pursue the American Dream through legitimate means.

Thus, we conclude this chapter by arguing emphatically that for many of the men and women who are currently incarcerated in our burgeoning prison system, the solution is access to quality drug treatment programs. The availability of successful drug treatment programs would produce several positive outcomes for the people like the men and women we interviewed.

1. Especially for first time possession offenders, drug treatment could be offered instead of incarceration. This would dramatically reduce the size of our prison population and would limit all of the negative outcomes associated with incarceration for the individual and his or her family.
2. Drug treatment, if successful, would significantly reduce recidivism, which would also have a significant impact on the overall size of our incarcerated population.
3. Drug treatment, if successful, should reduce the amount of property and personal crime that is committed by addicts who are attempting to feed a habit. This would improve public safety for all of us.
4. Drug treatment, if successful, would reduce individuals' reliance on expensive social welfare programs, thus allowing our society to focus these resources where they are most needed.

None of our recommendations are particularly groundbreaking, so why has this approach not been pursued? As many others, including Wright (1997) and Wacquant (2001), have argued, drug laws were established not in order to reduce drug use but rather to cordon off and remove unwanted individuals from society. In short, they both suggest that drug use poses significantly less of a threat to public safety than other crimes for which people are incarcerated. Second, as articulated by Nick, drugs are addictive and thus if introduced into a community there will be guaranteed—and quick—results. When the flow of drugs in to a community is unchecked and this phenomenon is coupled with laws that demand long mandatory minimum sentences for drug possession, an easily accessible pathway or mechanism is created to remove "undesirable" individuals—primarily low-income African American men—from society for long periods of time and with the very high probability of creating a revolving door of addiction and recidivism that will ensure that these individuals will spend most of their adult lives in prison. Perhaps this suggestion seems a bit over the top, yet when we consider the effectiveness of drug treatment—approximately 80 percent of cocaine users greatly reduced their addiction to it after three months of treatment and 50 percent were completely cocaine-free after treatment[12]—it is hard not to wonder why effective drug treatment programs are rarely offered to first-time offenders and instead they are remanded to prisons for upwards of eight to ten years for simply possessing substances like crack.

Secondly, we wonder why the majority of the bans on social welfare target drug offenders. If we, as a society, were interested in their successful reentry we would not create so many barriers to the establishment of a simple subsistence existence—stable housing, food security, and employment. Coupling treatment in lieu of prison and removing the bans on social welfare that apply to drug felons should have powerful and positive results. Why, we ask, should Lyman Sykes—and his family—endure three decades of prison, when perhaps alternative approaches might have allowed him to develop much earlier into a productive citizen and thoughtful parent whose responsibility for himself and his family would have saved tax payers the *hundreds of thousands of dollars* it cost to incarcerate him and provide welfare support to his family? We turn next to a discussion of another revolving door: the intergenerational cycle of sexual abuse.

Notes

1. www.whitehousedrugpolicy.gov/publications/factsht/druguse/.

2. This distinction is important for both "Three Strikes You're Out" and for bans that we will discuss later in the chapter.

3. http://bjs.ojp.usdoj.gov/content/glance/drug.cfm.

4. http://bjs.ojp.usdoj.gov/content/glance/drug.cfm.

5. For a good background report on the specifics of women in prison, especially for the period of the last two decades of the twentieth century, see the essay by Meda Chesney-Lind entitled "Imprisoning Women: The Unintended Victims of Mass Imprisonment," in Marc Mauer and Meda Chesney-Lind, eds., *Invisible Punishment: The Collateral Consequences of Mass Imprisonment*, pp. 78–94 (New York: The New Press).

6. Tragically Dana Plato died of her untreated cocaine addiction.

7. www.drugpolicy.org/drugwar/mandatorymin/crackpowder.cfm.

8. The reader will recall that we briefly introduced Nick in chapter 2.

9. www.forces.org/articles/files/whiteb/white01.htm.

10. http://mentalhealth.samhsa.gov/publications/allpubs/homelessness/.

11. William was a true southern gentleman who believed that women shouldn't have to work outside the home and that men should be able to provide. This explains his willingness to keep his sister in an apartment but not his brother.

12. http://books.google.com/books?id=HtGb2wNsgn4C&pg=PA240&lpg=PA240 &dq= percent25+average+success+rate+of+of+cocaine+abusers+in+the+U.S.&source= bl&ots=jlo6mjuWWM&sig=dquGEsRNkaqgyY6H8tNn6mazcbg&hl=en&ei=jiZZSv OqEIOltgf6rLDdCg&sa=X&oi=book_result&ct=result&resnum=1.

4

The Role of Sexual Abuse in Childhood

Research on women's criminality has brought to the forefront the relevance of childhood victimization. . . . Economic deprivation, social exclusion, desperation, and sexual vulnerability become part of the context of lived experiences that may generate further criminal activity as runaway girls cope with exposure to dangerous risks on the street. . . . Yet violent men and boys have also endured childhood victimization, neglect, and abuse. What makes this aspect of context unique for women? As Chesney-Lind and Pasko noted, "unlike boys, girls' victimization and their response to that victimization is specifically shaped by their status as young women." (Wesely 2006:305)

THIS CHAPTER FOCUSES ON THE TROUBLING RELATIONSHIP between childhood sexual abuse and the perpetration of sexual violence in adolescence and adulthood. As many researchers (Eisenberg, Owens et al. 1987; Hibbard and Zollinger 1990; Holmes and Slap 1998) argue, though sexual abuse has been widely studied among girls and young women (Hanson 1990; Pipher 1994; Holmes and Slap 1998; Raphael 2004) and the relationships between childhood sexual abuse (CSA) and negative consequences in adulthood—including drug addition and higher rates of suicide (Pipher 1994), involvement in prostitution and the sex trade (Raphael 2004), the criminal justice system (Goodkind, Ng et al. 2006), and risk for being battered in adulthood (Hattery 2008)—are widely documented, little is known about the negative consequences of CSA on boys. Holmes and Slap (1998) argue that the relative silence surrounding CSA among boys has fostered the belief "that the problem is uncommon and the consequences are not severe" (Holmes and Slap 1998).

In this chapter we will focus on the experiences of two men we interviewed for whom the consequences *were severe*: both were sent to prison by the time they were eighteen years old for raping and sexually abusing young girls.

CSA among Boys

Karen Terry and Jennifer Talon of John Jay College conducted an extensive review of the literature on sexual abuse (2004) in which they identify many of the critical elements to understanding male child sexual abuse—both for men as victims and men as offenders. Their report documents that one of the key issues in understanding CSA among boys is the inability of government agencies and researchers to accurately estimate the rate or prevalence of CSA among boys. Why? Boys are far less likely to report child sexual abuse, especially the abuse that occurs in adolescence. As a result, the best estimates we have range from 4 percent (MacMillan, Fleming et al. 1997) to 16 percent (Finkelhor 1990).

Regardless of the pitfalls in attempting to estimate the prevalence of child sexual abuse among boys, we can hypothesize that there are a host of negative consequences for the victims and that they mirror the types of consequences we see in female victims. Indeed, in their extensive review of the literature, Holmes and Slap (1998) note that just like girls, male victims of CSA are more likely than their non-victim counterparts to attempt and/or commit suicide and to use and abuse drugs. Critical to our argument, they also report that male victims of CSA are five times more likely than their non-victim peers to report "sexually related problems" and were 4.4 times more likely to report that they had "forced someone into sexual contact" (Holmes and Slap 1998).

Being a male victim of CSA, though it increases the risk that one will perpetrate sexual abuse in adulthood, does not automatically lead to this type of behavior. As figure 4.1 demonstrates, boys who are sexually abused in childhood are equally as likely to grow up to perpetrate sexual abuse as to not. Furthermore, there are many cases of sexual abuse perpetrated by men who were not sexually abused as children. That said, the risk for perpetrating sexual abuse as an adult is strongly shaped by one's experiences (or not) with sexual abuse in childhood. Thus, understanding sexual abuse in childhood as a pathway toward becoming an adult perpetrator is fundamentally important.

Brandon and Eddie

When we met Brandon he was twenty-one years old and had just been released from prison, having served twenty months on a twenty-six-month sentence for third-degree rape. Brandon was convicted at age nineteen of raping

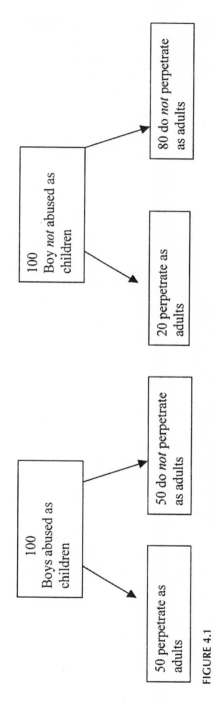

FIGURE 4.1
Relationship between CSA in childhood and perpetrating sexual abuse in adulthood

a thirteen-year-old girl. At the time of the interview Brandon was living in a homeless shelter and is a registered sex offender.

When we met Eddie he was twenty-four years old and had just been released from prison. Though he was most recently incarcerated for drug charges and probation violation, like Brandon, when Eddie was sixteen he was incarcerated for a year in a juvenile facility for felony rape of a minor. Also, like Brandon, at the time of the interview Eddie was living in a homeless shelter. In fact, he was about to be "evicted" because the time limit (thirty days per stay) was about to expire. He is also a registered sex offender.

As sociologists, one of the things we are trying to explain is how young men like Brandon and Eddie can have served prison terms for sexual violence and be registered sex offenders before either was twenty-two years old. What forces in their individual lives coalesced to create this trajectory? Though there are many different factors that intertwined to contribute to the pathway of each of their lives, several critical elements emerge in what turned out to be two remarkably similar experiences. About the only difference between them is their race: Brandon is African American and Eddie is White.

Brandon's early life was spent living with his mother, his younger brother, and his grandparents. Brandon had no relationship with his father, other than "he's the guy who signed my birth certificate." Unable to raise two boys on her own and make ends meet, his mother moved her family in with her parents. Brandon's memory of this time in his life is fairly happy; he had a good relationship with his grandfather and they lived a fairly comfortable middle-class life.

Despite these early "feel good" memories, when we asked Brandon "When was the first time you got in trouble?" he responded: "My very first time is unbelievable, really. I was eight years old. I was in the second grade." [AH: What did you do?] "An assault charge—I hit my guidance counselor with a golf club." Brandon was expelled from school for the first time in the second grade. For the next seven or eight years Brandon was constantly in and out of trouble, primarily for petty theft, selling drugs, running away, and assault. He was expelled repeatedly from school and by the tenth grade was not attending school at all. At age thirteen his mother remarried and moved the family to another part of town. According to Brandon he never really lived at home after that. Not having anywhere else to go, Brandon lived on and off the streets and "with friends."

Brandon explained his running away as due to a lot of fighting with his mother and his stepfather. He admitted that he was jealous and that it felt like his mother was spending more time with her new husband than with him and he felt neglected. Jealousy was clearly the underlying cause of the arguments, though the content was usually about his behavior. In his words, "I felt like there was no point in arguing no more—we're not going to agree on something and I'll just leave instead of fighting."

Brandon later revealed that he was not the only one doing the fighting; in fact his stepfather was beating his mother and was "physical" with him. At age thirteen Brandon was being beaten by his stepfather and, in addition, Brandon would often get in physical fights with his stepfather in an attempt to protect his mother. Eventually his mother and stepfather divorced, and Brandon actually moved home for a period of time.

For the majority of Brandon's relatively short life he has been in a variety of trouble ranging from school expulsion to jail sentences for assault. It was clear that Brandon is a very angry young man. The more we explored this anger with Brandon, the more clear it became that he was a victim of child sexual abuse at the hands of his stepfather and most likely by other men whom his mother dated across Brandon's childhood.

As noted by Holmes and Slap (1998), male victims of CSA are more likely to report "sexually related problems." When Brandon was about seventeen or eighteen he had exhausted places to stay and gotten tired of living on the streets. While selling drugs in the downtown area of the city Brandon started "talking" to a woman he described as "older"—she was thirty-two years old—and she invited him to move in with her. Though technically Brandon was an adult (or nearly so), this type of age difference involving a teenager and an adult is what we refer to as "premature sex engagement."[1] Premature sex engagement refers to having one's first and/or early sexual experiences as a teenager with a much older adult—someone who is at least ten years older than the child or adolescent.

Though these circumstances fit the definition of statutory rape, men and women we have interviewed across several projects (Hattery and Smith 2007; Hattery 2008) generally defined these experiences as "consensual." The issue of consent in these cases is a tricky and complex one (Odem 1995), which is reflected in recent moves by some states to modify their statutory rape laws to require age differences of at least a year; for example sex between two seventeen-year-olds no longer meets the legal requirements of statutory rape.

In Brandon's case, having a sexual relationship at age seventeen with a woman in her early thirties (she was thirty-two) is not only problematic with regards to the power differentials associated with age and experience, but also likely be related to his experience as a victim of CSA.

This issue is further complicated by the blurring of the term "consent" (Scully 1990). Research on incest and CSA notes that in many cases victims do report "consenting." And, this is particularly problematic with regards to the cases involving young boys and older women. For example, only recently have we given these cases any attention and treated them as criminal. And, the reasons for our inattention are important and revealing. First, our rigid and hegemonic notions of masculinity and sexuality (Connell and Messerschmdt 2005; Kimmel 2005) characterize men of all ages, and particularly young men, as being hypersexual: always desiring sex, always ready for a sexual encounter. Within the confines of this hegemonic construction of masculine sexuality it is virtually *inconceivable* that a young man could have sex when he didn't want to. And, it is inconceivable that a boy would report such an interaction for not only would he face disbelief but such an admission would damage his masculine identity. Second, and related, is the fact that we have constructed gender relations (Connell and Messerschmdt 2005; Kimmel 2005; Friedman and Valenti 2008) in such a manner as to restrict, at least in our commonly held ideology, such that we believe that men relate to women only through sex. Thus, it is not thought to be unusual that a young boy would have sex with his teacher, for example; in fact this type of relationship is normalized through its frequency of invocation in music videos, movies, TV shows, and pornography. We are taught, what young boy doesn't fall in love with and want to have sex with a teacher sometime during adolescence? Thus, when these incidents occur they are doubly likely to be met with disbelief and probably more often than in the reverse and are never reported. Yet, in the last fifteen years the news has been flooded with reports of women, often teachers, having sex with young men Brandon's age and younger. And, as a result, the criminal justice system has had to respond. We can only hope that this response will lead to greater attention to male victims of CSA and interventions and therapy for these victims so that they grow up without the predispositions for negative behavior—drug and alcohol abuse, sexual difficulties, and so forth—that past victims have been vulnerable to.

Brandon's situation illustrates all of the problems associated with premature sex engagement: he defined it as consensual, as a result of his experience with sexual abuse by a male he likely felt that a sexual encounter with an older woman affirmed his masculine and heterosexual identity, and as a result he never thought to "report" the incident; in fact he never seems to have questioned it.

Brandon had been living with this older woman for about three months when his cousin called him. Brandon's mother had discouraged Brandon from spending much time with this cousin because he was in and out of prison and she didn't want Brandon to be influenced by his cousin and/or get caught up in the same trouble. That said, after his cousin was released from prison he and his wife moved to Tacoma, Washington, and he claimed to have heard that Brandon was in trouble and he wanted to reach out and help. As a result of their conversation Brandon decided to move out to Tacoma and live with his cousin. Brandon hadn't been in Tacoma long when he realized that his cousin, who was married and living with his wife, was "picking up" much younger women. After dropping his wife of at work, Brandon's cousin, who was twenty-five years old, was cruising the Tacoma Mall and picking up twelve- and thirteen-year-old girls. His "game" was to identify a "cute" girl, offer to give her some drugs, and invite her to his apartment. Once there, he would give the girl some marijuana and/or beer and then take her in the bathroom and rape her. Brandon claims that at first he didn't know what was going on in the bathroom, but he simultaneously revealed that the apartment was a very small one-bedroom. Thus, it seems very unlikely that he didn't know.

Brandon revealed that one day his cousin called him and told him he had spotted a girl that was cute and perfect for Brandon. Along with his cousin, Brandon "picked up" the girl with the offer to give her some marijuana and beer. She got in the car and came home with Brandon and his cousin. Brandon claims that he thought she was sixteen years old (he was eighteen years old), but after he had sex with her, which he claims was consensual, she told her father, who pressed charges and Brandon was arrested for first-degree rape of a child and first-degree kidnapping: the girl was, in fact, only twelve years old. From Brandon's perspective he felt duped. He blamed the girl for representing herself as being older than she was. Eventually, after being held in jail for nine months, Brandon pled guilty to third-degree rape and was sentenced to twenty-six months in state prison. He served twenty-two months followed by forty-eight months on parole. After he was released from prison Brandon had his parole transferred back to North Carolina and he moved back to Winston-Salem.

Though Brandon's parole release was predicated on the fact that his mother had agreed to provide him with a place to live, after riding four days on a Greyhound bus, he arrived just as his mother was being evicted. She had decided to move in with her third husband, who had no interest in Brandon, a registered sex offender, joining their household, so Brandon moved into the homeless shelter.

In the eighteen months between Brandon's release from prison in Washington and our interview, he has struggled to get his life in order. After his time expired at the homeless shelter—men are allowed to stay only ninety days per "stint"—he moved first into a halfway house from which he was evicted for fighting, then in to a rooming house, from which he was evicted for fighting and getting behind on the rent; he slept on the couches of his friends, and returned more than once to the homeless shelter. His trajectory with employment has been similar. He has held a handful of legitimate jobs—working in local restaurants and fast food places—but has struggled to keep a job more than a few months because he is constantly getting in fights with the other staff, customers, or in one case some guys he was fighting with on the streets came one night to settle the score at the ice cream shop where he was working. As a result, he has gotten back into selling drugs and was arrested just before we interviewed him for robbing a home. He was facing a five-year prison sentence if convicted on that charge. As we were ending the interview with Brandon we asked him about his hopes and dreams. He is twenty-one years old and we wondered where he anticipated his life going. He mentioned planning to finish his GED and then taking classes in business. He wants to open a retail clothing store and sell his own designs. When we last checked in on Brandon, in the summer of 2009, we learned that he was once again back in jail, this time for violating the terms of his parole.

Eddie's early life was spent in an intact family, including his mother and father and siblings. Around age four or five his parents "split up" because Eddie's father was an alcoholic and would frequently beat up his mother. Like Brandon, he and his mother and his brother moved in with her parents, his grandparents. Eddie's mother was a prostitute and he recalled that by age seven or so he was aware of all the men that would come and go from his grandparents' house where she turned tricks. Besides describing it as "weird," Eddie also talked about the negative consequences of prostitution on children. Often the men passing through the home would beat on Eddie and his siblings and as he grew older, they would offer him drugs. Eddie was smoking marijuana with the "johns" by the time he was ten years old. Additionally, Eddie's mother didn't require her children to go to school. As a result, they didn't. Thus, another routine part of Eddie's life were the visits by the social workers who would try to enforce school attendance. Eddie recalled that when he was in elementary school, after each visit by the social worker, who also threatened to take custody of the children away from his mother, Eddie would go to school for a few days to "get her off my back" but soon after he would stop attending. Though literate, Eddie has probably not attended more than two cumulative years of school and by his teenage years he was not attending at all.

Between the ages of twelve and fourteen Eddie and his brother lived with their father, who refused to allow them to see their mother. Unfortunately Eddie traded one horrible family environment for another. When we asked Eddie about attending school while he was living with his father he responded that he attended whenever he didn't have bruises that were a result of being beaten, often with a belt, by his father. Though he complained repeatedly to social workers about being beaten and neglected neither he nor his brother were ever removed from the home.

Eddie's described his father as "crazy":

> But, I remember I come home one night and me and my brother had got the
> picture album and we was going through it and we was hungry. Dad knew—he

count every piece of bologna, he would count the pieces of bread, he would count everything. He was crazy. I mean you couldn't have nothing out of the ordinary. And, so, we was flipping through the picture album and we found one of them little sealed $5 bill—a little red ink $5 bill? I didn't think it was worth nothing, you know. I mean, a $5 bill, right there, *hungry time.* I took it and me and my brother went out to the store and bought some candy. When we got back we was munching down in our room and Dad come in there and got us. He beat the snot out of us. Went up to the store and got his $5 bill back, choked the owner of the store out, and acting crazy. I don't—my dad was gone crazy. He got the $5 bill back. He didn't get no charges or nothing. I don't know.

At age fourteen Eddie once again went back to living with his mother. At this point in the interview Eddie revealed the real reason he had gone to live with his father: his mother had married a man facing three child molestation charges. As a result, the court removed Eddie and his brother from her custody. Unfortunately this was much too late, as Eddie's stepfather had been molesting them for years. Eddie reluctantly, with downcast eyes, told in the briefest but most telling manner about the abuse.

> Eddie: But, I mean, I guess it's good to get it out. He messed with me when I was young and it feels messed up. It feels like, kinda, like you're gay or something because you—I don't know. It kinda feels like that though. Then you feel angry towards it like, I don't know.
>
> AH: Did your mom know?
>
> Eddie: I told her three times. She'd leave me there with him.

After Eddie and his brother were finally removed from their father's house by social workers they went to live with his father's mother, his grandmother. His grandparents were financially stable and lived in a nice house. Quickly, however, they grew tired of feeding two extra mouths and they relinquished custody of Eddie and his brother to an orphanage, where they lived for about six months. Eddie recalled that he really liked living in the orphanage, but apparently his grandmother started to feel guilty and she forced Eddie and his brother to move back in with her. Not long after, Eddie was charged with sexually molesting his younger cousin. Eddie was sixteen years old. He served a year in prison—at a youth detention center—was required to complete a sex offender treatment program, and register as a sex offender.

After serving a year in prison, Eddie was released and, having no one who would offer him a place to live, he moved directly in to the homeless shelter. He was seventeen years old. For the next several years Eddie was in and out of jail on minor drug charges and parole violations. During one of the stints when he was not locked up Eddie met a much older woman—he was nineteen years old and she was forty-five years old—who agreed to allow him to move in with her in exchange for sexual favors. And, though Eddie was clearly an adult and this relationship was not illegal, like Brandon his sexual experiences follow a similar pattern whereby most if not all of their sexual relationships take place with people who are either much older than they are or much younger; relationships in which sex is embedded inside of a relationship of clearly unequal power. In his own words, Eddie said that he engaged in this exploitative relationship because "I gotta survive."

Sometimes Eddie or Brandon were the victims and sometimes the perpetrators, but neither has any relationship of any length or importance that occurs with a peer, someone of their own age and status.

Among the sexual liaisons in Brandon's past, near the end of our interview with him Brandon revealed that at age sixteen he had been having casual sex with two different girls his own age. Both became pregnant within a few months of each other, and has a result, Brandon has a four-year-old son and a four-year-old daughter with two different women. Like many reentry felons, Brandon owes a tremendous amount of back child support to both women and he revealed that he had been back to court several times since being released from prison for his failure to pay child support. This, however, is the least of Brandon's problems as they concern his children. As a registered sex offender, and because he was never married to either of the mothers of his children, he is prohibited from having any contact with his children. Brandon indicated that his lawyer is "working on" getting permission from the court for him to be able to see his own children. But, even if that happens, there are other barriers he faces as a sex offender with regards to parenting. Sex offenders are banned from public housing. Both of his children live in public housing so Brandon would be prohibited from visiting them there. (He is also banned from living in public housing, which contributes to his struggles to find affordable housing.) Sex offenders are banned from being within 1,000 yards of a school. Thus, Brandon would not be allowed to have lunch with his children at school, attend open houses or parent teacher conferences or the school play or any of the other routine visits a parent makes to their children's elementary school. Sex offenders are prohibited from being within 1,000 yards of a park. Again, that means that even if Brandon could get a judge to allow him to visit his children, he would be prohibited from taking them to a local park to play. Given that he lives in transitional housing—homeless shelters, rooming houses, etc.—it seems likely that a park would be one of the most convenient places for someone like Brandon to spend time with his children.

The Cycle of Sexual Abuse

This book is not about trying to diagnose pedophilia or make broad claims about the cycle of sexual abuse. In order to make such claims we would have had to study many more individuals than we did. Furthermore, there is a solid scientific literature devoted to this type of analysis (Turvey 1996; Colton, Roberts et al. 2009). That said, we can use the data in our interviews to make some observations about what some men say about the cycle of sexual abuse.

I Didn't Do It!

In comparison to all of the other people we interviewed, Eddie and Brandon were insistent that they had not engaged in the sexually abusive behavior that they were charged with and convicted of. In both cases, they admitted that the sexually abusive behavior had occurred, but they argued that someone else had committed the abuse. Eddie claimed that it was actually his brother who had sexually abused his cousin and Brandon argued that it was actually his cousin who raped the twelve-year-old girl. Though many convicts, while they are on the inside, deny that they committed the crimes they were convicted of, in our experiences interviewing and working with reentry felons, once they are released and once they are convinced that a researcher is required to keep any information confidential, subjects are generally willing to admit what they have done. In some cases they even embellish it. One person we interviewed wove a story that seemed to suggest he was operating at the level of the biggest drug pins or mafia in history (Llee, whose story was presented in chapter 3). Yet, in both of the cases in which men were charged with sexually abusive behavior, both insisted, repeatedly, that it was not they who had committed the offense, but it was someone else close to them who had committed the offense. Thus, there is something different about the men convicted of sexual abuse of minors than their peers who were convicted primarily of nonviolent drug offenses and property crimes. Additionally we remind the reader that both Eddie and Brandon readily admitted to other kinds of behavior including assault, drug possession, and robbery.

Need to Assert Heterosexual Identity

Another theme that emerged from the interviews with Eddie and Brandon was the notion that as victims of childhood sexual abuse each young man had responded to this abuse by wondering and perhaps in the case of Eddie even worrying about their sexual orientation. We suspect that this was a far more profound concern for Eddie because the abuse he experienced was far more severe, occurred at a younger age, and lasted for a longer period of time. Additionally, the abuse Eddie experienced took place in a highly charged heterosexual and sexual environment: in the same house where his mother was working as a prostitute. Thus, Eddie's own evaluation of the sexual abuse he experienced was filtered through the lens of *hyper-heterosexual sex*. This combination, sexual abuse by a male and the context of heterosexual prostitution, led Eddie to reflect: "It feels like, kinda, like you're gay or something because you—I don't know. It kind feels like that though. Then you feel angry towards it like, I don't know."

Though the research on pedophiles includes discussions of both same and opposite sex abuse, the experiences of the men we interviewed seem to suggest that as victims of same-sex sexual abuse they sought out ways during adolescence to establish a heterosexual identity. This both took the form of sexually abusing young female victims and also can be seen in their other sexual activity. The reader will recall that both Eddie and Brandon had sexual relationships as teenagers with women who were not only much older than they were but these sexual arrangements were built on an economic exchange (see Hattery 2008). Both Eddie and Brandon were homeless teenagers who found older women who would provide shelter and food in exchange for sex. As noted above, this is very similar to the pattern of premature sex engagement that we describe in our other research (Hattery and Smith 2007; Hattery 2008; Hattery 2009). Finally, we remind the reader that Brandon also engaged in promiscuous, high-risk sexual behavior as a teenager: he was having sex with two teenage girls at the same time and both became pregnant within a few months of each other. Thus, our work suggests not only that male victims of CSA risk repeating the cycle of sexual abuse as perpetrators but also that their need to affirm their own sexuality as *heterosexual males*, particularly if they were abused by male perpetrators, resulted in both high-risk and exploitative sexual behavior in adolescence.

Sentences for Sex Offenders

One of the more perplexing problems we have noted in our vast examination of the criminal justice system as well as in our research with ex-offenders is the disparity in the sentences handed down to sex offenders as compared to others, including drug offenders convicted only of possession offenses. According to the Bureau of Justice Statistics, the average sex offender is sentenced to eight years in prison and serves, on average, only three and a half years. In contrast, because of mandatory minimum sentencing laws and requirements to serve at least 85 percent of the sentence for drug offenders (as detailed in chapter 3), the average felony drug offender is sentenced to ten years and is required to serve eight and a half. Our interviews confirmed both of these trends. The average drug offender we interviewed reported sentences and time served that were consistent with the law. And, as the reader will recall, both Eddie and Brandon served sentences that were less than two years.

As researchers and citizens not only are we concerned about the relatively short sentences that child molesters serve, but also this is especially troubling when we examine the disparity between the approaches to sentencing child molesters and drug offenders—most of whom are sentenced for possession, not for selling. Additionally, we must understand the experiences of Eddie and Brandon in this context. When we consider the impact of CSA on young men, especially the likelihood of repeating the cycle of abuse and/or engaging in other high-risk sexual behavior, we must conclude that as a society, our inability to hold perpetrators of child sexual abuse accountable increases the total number of children that are victimized and contributes to the consequent outcomes including the continuation of the cycle of sexual abuse as well as other high-risk sexual behavior that we see in the cases of Brandon and Eddie.

Recidivism for Sex Offenders

For a variety of reasons, including short sentences, the lack of access to treatment, and the relatively unsuccessful nature of treatment for sex offenders, especially those who abuse children, recidivism rates are exceptionally high. Again, according to the Bureau of Justice Statistics when compared to non–sex offenders, sex offenders are four times more likely to be re-arrested for a sexual offense and 40 percent of these re-arrests occurred within twelve months of release and within fifty miles of the original crime (Langan, Schmitt et al. 2003). Unfortunately, these statistics suggest that Eddie and Brandon are likely to engage in repeat sexually abusive behavior that is criminal—they meet every criterion for sex offenders who will recidivate including lack of treatment and relatively short sentences. Additionally, our interviews with these young men suggest that they face a high probability of engaging in non-criminal but high-risk and exploitative behavior, which creates negative consequences for both these young men and also for their sexual partners.

Unintended Consequences: Accumulated Advantages for Communities

Clearly we would not advocate that sex offenders who also happen to be parents be released from the restrictions that are designed to create a higher degree of public safety. In fact, we argue that one of the positive outcomes of incarceration, especially in low-income neighborhoods, is that locking up dangerous individuals, who are most likely to live in low-income neighborhoods, can have the effect of creating safety in neighborhoods that are otherwise plagued by a variety of problems that render them unsafe. For example, if sex offenders were allowed to live in public housing, then we would expect that they would. Why? For the simple fact that all reentry felons, and sex offenders in particular, struggle to find housing after they are released from prison. The struggle to find housing is strongly connected to the difficulties reentry felons have in finding stable employment. As a result, because of the relative affordability of public housing, reentry felons who are not banned from public housing would be likely to seek housing in these communities.

Research on low-income neighborhoods (Wilson 1984, 1987) demonstrates that these communities suffer from a variety of other problems that make their residents particularly vulnerable to criminal activity. So, for example, children in low-income neighborhoods are more likely to live in single-parent households, which increases the likelihood that they will be "latch key" children—arriving home alone and spending as many as several hours by themselves waiting for their parent or guardian to arrive home from work. Secondly, they are more likely to attend under-resourced schools that cannot afford to provide after-school programming like tutoring or sports (Thomas 2009). Thirdly, the unemployment rate in low-income communities tends to be double or triple that of the local average, and this is even more true if the neighborhood is primarily comprised of African Americans. African American men's unemployment rate is often four or five times the local and national averages (McGeehan and Warren 2009). Coupled together, this leaves children living in low-income neighborhoods more vulnerable to exploitation such as being offered drugs, being lured into prostitution, and being sexually abused and molested by older teenagers, unemployed men, and sex offenders. Thus, we can argue that the kinds of prohibitions that make it more difficult for Brandon to establish a relationship with his children, as troubling as they may be to him personally, are designed to reduce the negative consequences and greater risks that would otherwise be posed to citizens living in public housing neighborhoods—especially children. Thus, incarceration and prohibitions on certain types of reentry felons may have an accumulated advantage for those living in the communities sex offenders are most likely to come from and return to after incarceration. The price that we pay for this, however, is born by the reentry felons and by their families who often express a desire for their loved ones—their fathers, sons, and husbands—to return to the homes they left behind when they went to prison.

Conclusion

In this chapter we have explored the relationship between childhood sexual abuse and the perpetration of sexual abuse in adulthood by examining the experiences of two sex offenders whom we interviewed, Eddie and Brandon. When we analyze their experiences we find several disturbing trends:

(1) Male victims of childhood sexual abuse are at risk for repeating the cycle by engaging in sexual abuse themselves.
(2) Male victims of sexual abuse are at risk for engaging in other high-risk sexual behavior including multiple sex partners and unintended pregnancy.
(3) Male victims of sexual abuse are at risk for homelessness both as a result of trying to escape the abuse—as Brandon did as a teenager—and when they return as registered sex offenders following a conviction and period of incarceration.
(4) As a result, male victims of sexual abuse are at risk for entering consensual but exploitative relationships with significantly older women in order to secure access to housing and food.

These findings suggest that male victims of childhood sexual abuse are at risk for engaging in all kinds of behavior that put them in danger but most importantly put them at risk for repeating the cycle of sexual abuse, which, if caught, will lead to their incarceration and the requirement that they register as sex offenders.

Among the many problems these young men face is the balancing act that pits their individual self-interests against the self-interests of larger communities and society at large. Brandon's situation is a case in point. Though we have no way of guaranteeing that he would not sexually abuse either of his children, the barriers that he faces as a sex offender to establishing a relationship with his children are tremendous and it is most likely that he never will. Though absentee fathers in no way create the same risk and negative outcomes as abusive fathers, Brandon's absenteeism can create negative outcomes for his children, especially if he is also unable to find employment and contribute to their economic needs. This is especially problematic if the likelihood that he will be sexually abusive is small.

Primarily in response to especially horrific cases of child abduction, molestation, and homicide, the United States has responded by enacting legislation such as Megan's Law, which imposes severe restrictions on the liberties of released sex offenders through the system of sex offender registry. And, though we may feel safer as a result of the sex offender registry and restrictions on the presence of sex offenders in parks and near schools, the data on sex offenses tells a different story: namely that the rate of recidivism is tremendously high in spite of our best efforts to break the cycle of repeat offenses through these laws.

Quite perplexing to us is the fact that juxtaposed against these tremendously restrictive policies for sex offenders, the sentences imposed on sex offenders are extremely short and the percentage of sentences served is extremely small, especially in comparison to those imposed on and served by drug offenders. This raises the question of how seriously in fact we do treat sexual offenses in the U.S. criminal justice system. It appears that we treat sex offenses very lightly at all stages of the system until sex offenders are released back into society. Perhaps a better approach to reduce the likelihood that sex offenders will become re-offenders would be to treat sexual abuse far more seriously during all phases of the criminal justice process and not simply after offenders are released. Certainly the victims of sexual abuse and community members at large should expect sex offenders to be treated at least as severely as those convicted of possessing minimal amounts of crack or cocaine. Lastly, we note that there is very little attempt to offer effective treatment to sex offenders during their periods of incarceration. Perhaps if we required sex offenders to successfully complete rigorous and scientifically supported treatment protocols before release we would be able to reduce the likelihood of recidivism and ultimately reduce the number of victims of these heinous crimes.

We close the chapter by asking how we balance Brandon's (or Eddie's) individual interests and liberties against those of the larger community. We argue that there at least two key issues that must be considered: (1) the relationship between CSA and the perpetration of sexual abuse and (2) the accountability and treatment of sex offenders.

The Relationship between CSA and Perpetration of Sexual Abuse

As the cases of Eddie and Brandon so aptly point out, when male childhood sexual abuse takes place victims are created. When these victims are not recognized and their abuse is not addressed—through legal means, civil means, and treatment—the likelihood that these boys will grow up to become perpetrators themselves is high. Thus, the disservice we do is not only to the victims themselves but also to the potential victims in our communities. By not taking sexual abuse, especially of boys, seriously, the likelihood that sexual offenses will continue to grow is high and the potential negative consequences are great. Additionally, as illustrated in the cases of Eddie and Brandon, not only are male victims of CSA at risk for becoming perpetrators, but they are also at risk for other serious problems, including high-risk sexual activity, vulnerability to exploitative sexual relationships, homelessness, drug and alcohol abuse, and other criminal behavior.

The Accountability and Treatment of Sex Offenders

As noted, the recidivism rate of sex offenders is among the highest rates of recidivism of all types of offenders. We point out two key recommendations that might lower recidivism: accountability and treatment. As noted above, sex offenders serve relatively and ridiculously short sentences for crimes that result in profound and troubling consequences for the victims. Additionally, there are relatively few treatment programs available to sex offenders and even fewer that are successful. By not holding sex offenders accountable and by not investing in the development of successful treatment programs that are then made available to sex offenders we create a situation in which the likelihood of recidivating is high and we leave ourselves, our families, and our communities at unnecessary risk for victimization. In the next chapter we will turn our attention to the special case of the incarceration of women.

Note

1. See especially A. Hattery (2008), *Intimate Partner Violence* (Lanham, MD: Rowman & Littlefield); and A. Hattery (2009), "Sexual Abuse in Childhood and Adolescence and Intimate Partner Violence in Adulthood among African American and White Women," *Race, Gender and Class* 15(2): 79–97.

5

The Special Case of Women

I am a daughter, a sister, a mother of four children, a classical pianist and teacher, a drug addict, a felon, and inmate #N87420 of the Illinois Department of Corrections. . . . My crime is considered a victimless one, but I say, there are no victimless crimes. My family, my children and I are the victims of my crime. My crime is a disease; the disease of addiction—cunning, baffling and powerful. . . .

Let me clearly state I am not saying addicts who commit crimes should go unpunished. I do believe, however, alternatives to incarceration are more cost effective. Programs that stress rehabilitation, allows the offender an opportunity to reenter society as a responsible and productive citizen. . . . The prison system has become a revolving door for drug offenders. Upon serving their sentence, they are released back into the same environment from which they came, without any skills or education to change their situation. Often the knowledge they have gained in prison is better ways to commit more crimes. Oftentimes, (I have experienced this myself) women are thrown into whatever programs are provided by the State or DOC, regardless of whether these programs meet the particular needs of the offender. Obviously, for all our time, effort, and money, we are no closer to solving the problem of women committing crimes. Perhaps, what we need to do is simply go back to the basic—to reduce our treatment of women offenders to the lowest denominator, that of human and humane contact.

Instead of incarceration, I believe it would be more cost-effective to put women offenders in a community based program similar to the work release program that is used for prisoners after incarceration. (Schwartz 2004)

P RISONS ARE GENDERED INSTITUTIONS. Historically and through till the present day prisons are overwhelmingly populated by men. Across the history of the criminal justice system in the United States prison populations have remained consistently about 90 percent male and about 10 percent female. This is clearly reflected not only in the statistics on inmate populations but also with regards to prisons and jails structurally. In our home community, the new jail that was built a decade or so ago has eleven floors: ten for men and one for women. In a state like North Carolina, which has eighty-nine prisons, only five (5 percent) hold women inmates. Yet, for a variety of reasons, women as inmates pose unique and interesting questions for both those who specialize in incarceration and researchers who study women's experiences in prison as well as their experiences with reentry. We begin with some statistics on women's incarceration.

Statistics

Though women make up only 10 percent of the incarcerated population in the United States, they are the fastest-growing demographic group that is entering prison. In the last few years, the rate has been especially steep, notably for African American women. Sokoloff notes that nearly one million women are "under the control of the criminal justice system today," including more than 100,000 in prison, another 100,000 in jail, and 800,000 on parole and probation; more than half are African American (2003:32). In fact, over the last two decades, the incarceration rate for African American women alone has increased nearly 900 percent (O'Brien 2007). The probability that a woman will be incarcerated in her lifetime is now 11/1,000, or 1.1 percent[1] (Harrison and Beck 2005). And, just as the changes in drug laws have produced a substantial increase in the male inmate population (see our discussion in chapter 3), the impact has been even more dramatic for women. Mauer and Chesney-Lind note:

> Women in prison are considerably more likely than men to have been convicted of a drug offense. As of 1998, 34 percent of women offenders had been convicted of a drug offense, compared to 20 percent of men, and two-thirds have children under18. (Mauer and Chesney-Lind 2002:84–85)

Furthermore, when coupled with nonviolent property offenses, drug felonies account for nearly 80 percent of the female inmate population (Women in Prison Project 2006). Feminist criminologists also note gender disparities in sentencing, especially for crimes, such as murder (Browne 1989) and drug offenses (Edin and Lein 1997; Hattery and Smith 2007; Seccombe 1998) for which women receive sentences that are more severe than men who are convicted of the same crime under the same circumstances.

The relatively steep rise over the last thirty years in the incarceration of women has raised a whole new set of issues related to dealing with inmates. Most research on the criminal justice system notes that women have distinct needs, including pregnancy, childbirth, and parenting (Bloom, Owen, and Covington 2004; Britton 2003; Enos 2001; Golden 2005; Morash and Schram 2002; Morash 2006; Morash, Bynum, and Koonm 1998; Women in Prison Project 2006). Additionally, most incarcerated women are also victims of intimate partner violence; 78 percent report that they were abused by their intimate partners before entering prison (Islam-Zwart 2004). Our previous research (Hattery and Smith 2007), confirmed by other studies (Women in Prison Project 2006), documents a high correlation between incarceration and intimate partner violence for women. In some cases, women are incarcerated for murdering their abusive partners (Browne 1989; Women in Prison Project 2006). In others, their illegal behavior is related to the abuse they are subjected to, including drug and alcohol use often used as a coping mechanism or crimes related to their attempts to escape the abuse, most often property crimes and financial crimes (e.g., writing bad checks) (Hattery and Smith 2007; Women in Prison Project 2006).

Incarcerated Mothers

While obviously both men and women who go to prison may be parents—men leave approximately five million children behind—there are significant and unique challenges that shape mothers' incarceration experiences differently than fathers. For starters, approximately 75–80 percent of incarcerated women are mothers of *minor children*, averaging 2.11 children under the age of eighteen each for a total of at least a million children whose mothers are incarcerated (Enos 2001; Greenfeld, and Snell 1999). Second, compared to fathers (44 percent), the majority of mothers (64 percent) lived with their minor children immediately prior to their incarceration (Mumola 2000). Lastly, one key difference is that women can and do, at a rate of 6 percent, enter prison while pregnant.

Providing care and custody for their minor children is a main concern for most mothers who are incarcerated. The majority of the children of incarcerated mothers live with a grandparent (52.9 percent), 28 percent live with their fathers, and 25.7 percent live with another relative. The remaining 20 percent were placed in foster care or with "a friend" (Mumola 2000:1). In contrast, when fathers are incarcerated, in nearly all the cases (89 percent) the children lived with their mother and fewer than 2 percent were placed in foster care (Mumola 2000). Thus the stresses and challenges that mothers who are incarcerated face are far more complex than those faced by fathers. In short, fathers are less likely to face the types of legal custody battles that mothers face, a point we will return to later in this chapter. That said, mothers are more likely to report weekly contact with their children (60 percent) as compared to fathers (40 percent) (Mumola 2000:1), though as we will discuss later in chapter 6, contact, especially contact visits, carry their own associated stress. There are significant race differences with regards to maternal incarceration as well.

Race

The scant and recent literature on women in prison notes racial patterns that mimic those for men. Although African American women make up only 13 percent of the female population, they comprise more than half of all female inmates and are more likely to be incarcerated for drug offenses than White women[2] (Harrison and Beck 2005; Rolison, Bates, Poole, and Jacob 2002; Sokoloff 2003).

As the research on deviance in general and drug use in particular points out, perceptions of who uses drugs and beliefs about the relative seriousness of using different kinds of drugs can shape what offenses are reported to agents of the criminal justice system, how officers make arrests, and who prosecutors choose to prosecute. As noted in chapter 3, the crack-powder debate largely turns on this ideology. Thus, it is easy to see how differential treatment in the "free world" may account for some of these disparities in incarceration, especially for drug offenses. For example, studies of differential treatment of pregnant women find that regardless of *similar* or *equal* levels of illicit drug use during pregnancy, African American women are *10 times* more likely than White women to be reported to child welfare agencies for prenatal drug use (Chasnoff, Landress, and Barrett 1990; Neuspiel 1996).[3]

This racial disparity can only be explained by the power of hegemonic ideologies in shaping perceptions. Simply put, when a pregnant African American woman is discovered using drugs, this confirms our stereotype of African American women as crack heads, and therefore she and her children are referred to child welfare agencies or agents of the criminal justice system. In contrast, when a pregnant White woman is discovered using drugs, this appears to be an isolated event; it doesn't match the stereotype, and thus she is not referred to child welfare agencies or agents of the criminal justice system. Similar to racial profiling, the stereotype we hold about drug use and race are powerful in shaping the overall incarceration rates of African Americans and Whites.

Racial disparities with regards to the children of incarcerated mothers are profound. "Of the Nation's 72.3 million minor children in 1999, 2.1 percent had a parent in State or Federal prison. Black children (7.0 percent) were nearly 9 times more likely to have a parent in prison than White children (0.8 percent). Hispanic children (2.6 percent) were 3 times as likely as White children to have an inmate parent" (Mumola 2000:2). The fact that African American children are more likely to be placed in foster care than White or Hispanic children[4] indicates that more African American mothers have to seek legal means to regain custody of their children and more African American children whose mothers are incarcerated languish in foster care (Ross, Khashu, and Wamsley 2004), a point to which we will return later in this chapter.

Sameness/Difference Debate

One of the most important questions facing researchers and policymakers concerns *sameness and difference* among male and female inmates. The sameness/difference debate is a long-standing one in feminism. At the crux of the argument—a point that pits proponents of liberal feminism against those who embrace radical feminism—is the question of whether men and women have significant enough differences to be treated differently or whether men and women are just different versions of each other and thus treatment ought to be the same. Let us start with an example unrelated to incarceration. As we all know, both men and women participate in market labor; they are employed. One of the critical issues facing employees and employers is the issue of maternity leave and childcare. Liberal feminists argue that because until now at least only women experience pregnancy and childbearing, accommodations should be made to insurance policies and workplace practices that allow for women who are pregnant, nursing, or who have just given birth to complete these "tasks" without penalty as employees. Thus we have maternity leave policies, nursing rooms, and childcare support; of course the availability of these policies and practices varies greatly from employer to employer and the federal government refuses to require a reasonable universal standard for accommodations by employers. The only federally mandated policy, the Family and Medical Leave Act or FMLA, requires only that employers provide twelve weeks of *unpaid leave* and the assurance that an employee who takes such a leave to care for a family member who is ill or to welcome a new family member via birth or adoption will be able to return to his or her job after the twelve weeks. Additionally, FMLA is only mandated for employers with fifty or more employees.

In contrast, radical feminists reject the idea of modifying the workplace to accommodate female employees and instead advocate an entire modification to workplace demands and family life such that neither is incompatible with the other and both men and women will have the opportunity to participate in both spheres as they choose. Though far from complete, the family leave policies in Scandinavian countries approximate this perspective more closely; both men and women are offered identical parental leave and in fact maternity leave improves—both the amount of time and the percent of pay—when fathers take a leave as well. Scandinavians argue that these policies and practices create more equity at work *and* at home and that both institutions—workplace and family—are strengthened as a result.

In terms of incarceration, policymakers clearly recognize that there are some differences between male and female inmates with the key differences revolving around women's reproductive capacities. Yet, these "differences" rarely result in differential practices. Instead, the model in incarceration is to apply the concept of "sameness" and thus in an attempt to treat male and female inmates the "same" some unique and troubling practices have developed.

Pregnancy and Childbirth

As noted, approximately 6 percent of women entering state prison each year are pregnant at the time of their admission to a correctional facility. The majority of these pregnant women are sentenced to longer terms than the remainder of their pregnancy and thus the correctional institution must have a policy and set of practices for handling prenatal care, labor, and delivery. As with many other policies and practices inside correctional institutions there are few federal regulations and as a result there is wide variance across states and even within institutions under the same department of corrections. However, the majority of research, journalistic reports, and our own interviews confirm that the policies and practices are based on a "sameness" ideology that puts both mothers and their children at risk.

We interviewed Kezia, a thirty-something African American woman, about a year after she had been released from prison after serving a five-year sentence for possession of crack-cocaine. She was pregnant with her youngest child at the time she was first admitted to prison and she finished her pregnancy and delivered her child while incarcerated. Her experience mimics the majority of scholarly literature and journalistic accounts that address this issue and thus we use her case to illustrate what is a typical experience for pregnant inmates.

Kezia's Case

Kezia grew up in the housing projects in Winston-Salem and like so many poor, young African American women when she was a young teenager she started hanging around on the corner with older guys. She became sexually involved with these older men because she was bored, because it made her feel like an adult, and because these men, who were dealing drugs, had money. (See Hattery 2009 for a more in-depth discussion of what we term "premature sex engagement," the practice of older men engaging in the sexual exploitation of teenage girls, especially in low-income communities.) By the time she was sixteen years old she was a mother and by the time she entered prison in her mid-twenties she had four children and was pregnant with her fifth. The father of her children is a drug dealer who has been in and out of prison during all of the years Kezia has been involved with him. Essentially they live together when he is "free," she gets pregnant, and he is arrested for drug dealing and is sent back for another stint in the penitentiary. Like so many other women living in this environment filled with drugs, dealing, and the repeated cycle of incarceration, Kezia took "the wrap" for the father of her children. In an attempt to save the father of her children from a life sentence to be imposed under the Three Strikes You're Out or habitual felon law, during a raid on their apartment Kezia told officers that the drugs they found belonged to her and not to the father of her children. (See Hattery and Smith 2007; Hattery 2008, for a similar account.)

When Kezia was arrested and sent to prison she was about six months pregnant. She was initially sent to a women's prison in Raleigh, North Carolina, where the majority of women inmates in North Carolina are housed. Because she was sent to the largest women's prison in North Carolina and there were many other pregnant women there, she was housed in a unit specifically for pregnant women and women who had just delivered babies. There were at least two positive consequences to this. First, it facilitated the delivery of pre- and post-natal care and thus Kezia probably received better pre- and post-natal care than had she been housed in the general population or in a prison or jail without a unit such as this. Second, when she went in to labor there were other women who could help her. She recalls that when she was in the early stages of labor, not quite sure that it had officially begun, women who had recently given birth and those who had been incarcerated in the unit longer than she had directed her to immediately notify the guards so that she could be transported to the hospital for the remainder of her labor and delivery. Had they not given her this advice she suggested that she would have labored in her cell much longer without assistance or medical supervision.

What Kezia had not anticipated was the "sameness" approach that is at the core of the transport, labor, and delivery stages of pregnancy. As is standard practice in any transport of an inmate, laboring or not, Kezia was shackled for her trip to the hospital. Specifically she was put in handcuffs that were attached to a "belly chain" and her feet were put into leg irons that were then shackled together, the "inmate shuffle" her only way to move. Thankfully she was still in the early stages of labor, when contractions are milder; nevertheless any woman who has experienced labor would likely protest this action as one that not only would be uncomfortable but would also constitute inhumane treatment that would violate human rights treatises.

After being transported to the labor and delivery unit of the local hospital, as is standard practice with all inmates receiving treatment in a "free world" hospital, once in the bed, Kezia's hands were handcuffed to the rails and her ankles were shackled to the rails as well. (One of the authors recalls working in a hospital during summers in college and witnessing male inmates being shackled just this way as they waited for, completed, and recovered from angiograms.) The only "support" Kezia was allowed in her room during labor and delivery were the guards, stationed with pump shot guns, to be sure she didn't attempt to escape.

The logic behind this practice is that any foray into the "free world" by inmates presents an opportunity to escape. Thus, inmates are always shackled and guarded during any and all transport and during their stay in the "free world." The reader might recall seeing inmates transported this way in airports, on buses, or in hospitals or courtroom settings.

We understand the logic behind this practice for at stake is all of our public safety. An inmate's comfort must always be weighed against the likelihood that they pose an escape risk and the probability that if they were to escape this would threaten public safety. We wonder, though, about the practice of shackling pregnant women as they labor and deliver their babies. We are certain that any specialist in obstetrics would argue that this practice puts both the mother and the infant at risk for medical complications, especially the practice of shackling through the delivery. And, any woman who has had a baby and perhaps any man who has witnessed it would conclude that this practice constitutes cruel and unusual punishment and violates even those few human rights retained by inmates. We wonder, has the need to adhere to the principle of "sameness" gone too far in cases such as Kezia's and cases like hers that occur every single day in this country?

Post-delivery

Once a shackled mother in leg irons delivers her infant into the world and the medical staff have certified that mother and baby are "doing well," the baby is taken to the nursery and as soon as she is stable, often less than twenty-four hours after giving birth, the inmate mother is returned to the same corrections facility she left just hours before. Post-natal care, whatever that entails, is now in the hands of the prison medical staff. The baby is in temporary custody of the state and the mother has but twenty-four hours to make arrangements for a designated relative to take custody of the child from the neonatal unit.

When we interviewed Kezia we had read the literature and journalistic accounts and thus we were not surprised when she recounted that her child was taken away from her almost immediately—she barely saw her child—and that custody was turned over to a relative, in this case Kezia's mother. What we were not prepared for was the *process* that Kezia described. Kezia talked about how she was back in the women's prison just hours after she had given birth. Thankfully in Kezia's case because this was not her first birthing experience she knew what to expect in terms of post-partum bleeding and care. But, we wondered about the first-time mother who is forced to return to a prison cell with little access to supplies and perhaps less access to advice about how to ease the first few days after giving birth. Would she know about "Tucks" and the other remedies women rely on to ease the pain of an episiotomy? Would she know how much post-partum bleeding was normal and when she should be concerned? Would she recognize the swelling in her breasts as her milk "coming in" and would she know what to do about it? But, we learned something even more disturbing from Kezia as she recounted the day her baby was born: we learned that the process for arranging for care for the infant is unnecessarily burdensome and in all likelihood results in more children being taken into foster care than necessary.

Kezia revealed that she was not allowed to begin the process of alerting her family members about the new baby until *after* she was returned to her cell in the corrections facility. Once she was safely back in prison, Kezia was allowed a fifteen-minute phone call to arrange for her mother to pick up her baby and take temporary custody of her. And, the twenty-four-hour period for the baby to be "claimed" had already begun ticking when the child was born. Kezia recalls having barely enough time to reach her mother, give her mother the necessary information about what hospital the baby was at, and for her mother to drive several hours to the hospital to take custody of the baby. Kezia had forgotten to tell her mother in this most important phone call that the baby was born with red hair. This would be an especially important fact because Kezia and the father of her children are both African American.

So, when her mother arrived at the hospital looking for Kezia's daughter she initially dismissed the child that the hospital claimed was Kezia's because the baby had red hair. By some miracle, Kezia's mother was able to place a phone call to the corrections facility and get confirmation that this was in fact Kezia's baby. Had any more unexpected events arisen or any more time passed, Kezia's daughter would have been placed in the foster care system as an "abandoned child."

Though Kezia had no answer, we wondered about the process of transferring custody of an inmate mother's baby. Why not allow the mother to call the designated family member *before* she left the correctional facility to labor and deliver the baby, thus giving the family member more time to make arrangements? Or, why not allow the mother—or even the hospital—to contact the designated relative immediately after the baby was born? What would happen to babies whose mothers were incarcerated half a day's drive from their extended family, as is very often the case in states like North Carolina, where inmates are typically housed in facilities far away from their home counties? We understand that there are public safety concerns. Perhaps the logic behind not allowing the inmate multiple phone calls is specifically designed to prevent the family members from arriving at the hospital while the inmate is still there and thus allowing contact between them. But, weighing the welfare of the child and the costs—financial and otherwise—associated with foster care against the requirements for "sameness" and public safety it is not at all clear that the policies and procedures are the most appropriate for all parties concerned. We suggest that the costs of treating women as if they are the same, at least in this case, are too high and contribute significantly and unnecessarily to the many negative consequences that children whose mothers are incarcerated experience.

What Happens to the Children?

Kezia's case illustrates the special circumstance when an inmate is pregnant while incarcerated. And, her case is critically important because it highlights some of the problems in policy and procedure that result from the "sameness" approach as well as some of the causes of the negative consequences for children whose mother is incarcerated. Yet, these cases occur only 6 percent of the time. Far more common and equally problematic are the policies and procedures that are designed to address the more common situation when mothers are incarcerated and they leave their minor children behind.

As is the case with labor and delivery, there are no federal or even state laws that govern the development of policies and procedures when mothers are arrested or sent to prison. The implementation of policies and practices are often left to the discretion of arresting officers, police departments, or individual corrections institutions and this increases the variation dramatically. That said, both the lack of any universal principles and the variation in specific implementation of policies and practices is troubling. So, for example, depending on the nature of the situation and the arresting officer's disposition, often when women are arrested they are not given any time to make arrangements for their minor children, even those who are living with them—which is the case more than 60 percent of the time. If a mother is not given any time to make arrangements, her minor children may be taken into custody alongside her—there are even some reported cases of situations in which toddlers and elementary school–aged children have been handcuffed—and transported either to the police station or to child protective services. We can only imagine the emotional and psychological impact on a child who witnesses such an event. The impact is compounded by the fact that the child may not have any idea where he or she is headed, who will designated his or her caregiver, where he or she will sleep that night and for many nights after that, or when he or she will be able to see the mother again. We as a society indicate that we are troubled by the intergenerational cycle of incarceration yet our policies and procedures work against our expressed goal to break the cycle. The lack of a standard and humane policy for dealing with minor children whose mother is being arrested is a case in point.

As noted previously, the majority of children whose mother is incarcerated are cared for by their grandmothers, but too many are also relegated to foster care. Either way, one of the primary hurdles many incarcerated mothers face is the struggle to retain legal custody of their minor children. For example, legal policies may *force* them to lose permanent custody.

> Reunification laws became more punitive in 1997 under the Adoption and Safe Families Act (ASFA), which states that if a mother does not have contact with a child for six months, she can be charged with "abandonment" and lose rights to her child. Likewise, if a child has been in foster care for fifteen of the prior twenty-two months, the state may begin proceedings to terminate parental rights. However, women are often transferred from one facility to another, thus missing important deadlines and court dates that can result in termination of their parental rights . . . the threat of losing their children is quite real. (Sokoloff 2003:35)

To most people, especially parents, it may seem totally reasonable that a mother (or father) could have their custody challenged if they went more than six months without having contact with their minor children. But, those people who have been incarcerated or whose family members have

been incarcerated know that maintaining contact can be extremely challenging and varies tremendously across a range of factors. For example, Beth
Richie, a sociologist who studied incarcerated women,[5] writes of her own
frustration driving several hours to the correctional facility where she had
arranged, through the corrections staff, to interview female inmates only
to be denied entrance on a particular day because the entire facility was on
lockdown. Or, arriving only to be told that the inmate she was scheduled to
interview had been transferred or was in the infirmary, or worse, the "hole."
This is a common experience for those of us who visit prisons for any reason:
research, teaching, volunteering, or to visit a loved one. Phone contact can
be equally as problematic. In many states the department of corrections has
an agreement with the local "Bell" company to provide phone service for
the inmates. In the majority of states—except in places like New York state
where there have recently been lawsuits settled—the inmates are charged
$3–4 *per minute* to make a call, which provides a steady source of revenue
for the department of corrections as well as "Bell." Thus, an inmate with very
little canteen money may simply be unable to make regular phone calls. In
many cases the number of phone calls per week and the length of each call
is doled out as part of a merit system. In the Mississippi State Penitentiary
at Parchman, for example, only those inmates who have been promoted to
"A or B custody" have phone privileges. Because all inmates are assigned to
"C custody" during their "orientation" period, which lasts until they behave
well enough to earn "B custody," it is not uncommon for inmates go long
stretches without phone privileges. Some former inmates we've talked to
recall that in some facilities inmates are allowed one fifteen-minute phone
call per week. If the person they are calling doesn't answer the phone they
are not allowed to "try again" or call someone else. And, because inmates are
generally not allowed to receive calls this is their only mechanism for staying
in phone contact. All of this, coupled with the examples Richie points out,
create a context in which it is actually very common for inmates to have a
six-month stint where they are out of contact with people in the "free world"
. . . including their children.

Though most of us in the "free world" would naturally assume that contact
visits would be the only way to survive the incarceration of a loved one, or our
own, often inmates and their families recount a different perspective. Many
currently incarcerated men as well as several ex-inmates, including exoneree
Mr. Darryl Hunt, have talked at length about how painful visits, both contact
and non-contact, can be. (Contact visits allow inmates and their visitors to
sit in the same room together and generally they are allowed some minimal
amount of physical contact such as sharing hugs and holding hands. Non-
contact visits refer to visits in which inmates and their visitors are separated

by a Plexiglas window and the conversation must take place through a phone that each person has at their seat.)

Visits can be difficult for many reasons, but inmates and former inmates offer some insight. Many incarcerated people don't want their family members and friends to see them "this way," in prison uniforms, handcuffed and shackled, and under the control of prison guards. Consider that in both contact and non-contact visits inmates may have their handcuffs removed but often their leg irons remain. Furthermore, even if their handcuffs and shackles are both removed for the visit it is not uncommon for their visitors to watch the process of moving the inmate into the visiting room fully handcuffed and shackled before the guard removes either or both. Inmates describe this as humiliating. And, they are often the most resistant to having their children see them in this context. Secondly, conversation can be awkward. Inmates generally want to talk about anything other than prison but visitors often want to focus the conversation on the incarceration in order to reassure themselves that their loved one is all right. Which, of course, generally demands that the inmate lie because no one is ever "all right" while in prison. What does one make small talk about when the penitentiary and the "free world" are so far removed from one another? Depending on the institution, custody level, and other factors, inmates may or may not have access to a television and even if they do they frequently have limited channels so even talking about mundane topics such as "American Idol" as a way to pass the visit may not be possible. Inmates and former inmates talk about how difficult it is to say goodbye at the end of the visit. This is often so painful and they often dread this so intensely that in the end they prefer not to have any visits at all. Lastly, there is a whole set of unique issues that apply when the visits allow contact.

In conversations with other researchers in this area as well as inmates and former inmates and their families, one of the issues that continues to come up involves the types of searches that are required for both the visitor and the inmate for each and every visit. When contact visits are allowed, be they in a room or in the case of conjugal visits in a trailer, both the inmate *and* the visitor(s) must endure significantly more security checks of their person. In many cases this involves a strip and body cavity search for the inmate and a significant pat down for the visitor. Many women inmates, in particular, report that the contact visits themselves are virtually ruined by the strip and body cavity searches, which are humiliating, an experience that is often intensified because they may be performed by male guards. Many women report that in the beginning they craved contact visits with their children, but over time they decided that the searches of both themselves and their children were too invasive and humiliating to be worth it. (For an excellent description of this process we recommend two books by Asha Bandele: *The Prisoner's Wife* and *Some Like Beautiful: One Single Mother's Story*.)

Visits of any kind may also be prohibitive for structural reasons and economic reasons. For example, fewer maximum-security prisons are available for women, so they are often incarcerated far from their homes (Chesney-Lind 1998); over 60 percent of mothers in prison are incarcerated more than one hundred miles from their children, making visitation financially prohibitive and often impossible (Bloom 1993; Krisberg and Temin 2001).

We provide an example. For one of our previous books we did a "thought experiment" in which we mapped the distance between the counties in North Carolina and the institutions that housed the majority of offenders (Hattery and Smith 2007). Our experiment revealed that in a state like North Carolina the majority of inmates come from one part of the state but the majority are housed in another, typically rural, mountainous, and less accessible, county. Thus, family members from a coastal county, where rates of incarceration are very high, would have to travel several hundred miles to the mountain counties of the west in order to visit correctional facilities where thousands of inmates are held. If the family doesn't have a car, which we know from our research is common, they would likely have to rely on bus transportation. In researching for our thought experiment we learned that a bus ticket from a coastal city like Jacksonville to a mountain county with a prison, like Avery County, costs $87 *one way* and the trip takes eight to ten hours *each way*. For many low-income families both the cost and the time may prohibit more than a few visits per year. And, recall what we noted earlier: it is not uncommon to arrive for the visit and the inmate is for some reason not allowed to visit that day or he may have even been transferred to another facility without having a chance to contact his family.[6] Thus, especially for situations in which the term of incarceration is long, it may be nearly impossible for family members to commit to frequent and regular visits.

We do point out that at the time of this writing there are several innovative programs in a handful of states, including North Carolina, that are designed to reduce the barriers that inmate mothers face to mothering. These programs, all of which are in the development and trial stages, include cell blocks for mothers with infants—infants would be able to live with their mothers in prison until age two—halfway houses and pre-release programs for low-risk inmate mothers that would allow them to live with their children, and programs, such as Prison Girl Scouts, that facilitate regular, weekly visits—without the harassing body cavity searches—between daughters and mothers. We hope that these programs prove successful so that the negative impact of incarcerating mothers will be lessened.

Regardless of all of the difficulties in maintaining contact, the majority of inmates, and this is even more significantly true for women, will be released. And, upon release, the majority of reentry felons seek to reconnect with their families and often rely on their families for subsistence—a place to live and food to eat—especially in the first year post-release. (The reader will recall in chapter 3 we illustrated this with the case of the self-acclaimed "drug pin" Llee, who had to move back home to live with his mother after he was released from prison.)

There are two key issues related to reentry: becoming self-sufficient and reestablishing family life. We devoted chapter 2 to a lengthy discussion of the former, and therefore we focus on the latter here.

Reestablishing Family Life

Reentry theorists (Travis and Waul 2003) and researchers (Petersilia 2003) address the critical issue of reintegrating ex-prisoners back into their communities. However, at least for men, it is critical to point out that few were integrated into their respective communities at the time of arrest (Kurlychek, Brame, and Bushway 2006).

> Many of the women coming home must psychologically learn to deal with society and prepare for some level of rejection. . . . Often women are not immediately accepted back into their communities, or even their homes and families. Little things that everyday people take for granted become monumental tasks for a woman returning from even short periods of incarceration. (Willis 2005:A15)

Female inmates report that being separated from their children is the hardest part of their incarceration, contributing to problems in reestablishing family life post-release (Allard and Lu 2006; Women in Prison Project 2006). Mothers face added complications in the reentry process because though some may have had their parental rights terminated by the state while incarcerated, most seek to reestablish the mother role, regain custody, and provide for their children (Allard and Lu 2006; Women in Prison Project 2006). In order to do so, they must prove themselves fit and appropriate caregivers, including the establishment of a residence and a source of income, both of which are impeded by bans on social welfare.

We remind the reader that we engaged in a lengthy discussion of the social welfare bans that impede the reentry process in chapters 2 and 3. Because the majority of female inmates who are ultimately released back into the "free world" were convicted on felony drug charges, and these bans specifically target felony drug offenders, women, and especially African American women, face an unusually steep climb on the road to becoming self-sufficient. We refer the reader back to chapters 2 and 3, but offer a summary here. As a result of the federal welfare legislation of 1996, there is now a lifetime ban on the receipt of welfare for anyone convicted of a drug felony, unless a state chooses to opt out of this provision. As of 1999, eight states have chosen to opt out of the ban and another eighteen have modified it, such as exempting persons convicted of possession offenses, but half (twenty-four) the states are fully enforcing the provision, which means that drug offenders will have an even more difficult transition back into the community than reentry felons more generally (Mauer 2002).

Beth Richie (2001:381–82) sums up this problem nicely:

> The woman will need an apartment to regain custody of her children, she will need a job to get an apartment, she will need to get treatment for her addiction to be able to work, and initial contact with her children may only be possible during business hours if they are in custody of the state. The demands multiply and compound each other, and services are typically offered by agencies in different locations. Competing needs without any social support to meet them may seriously limit a woman's chances for success in the challenging process of reintegration.

Because African American women who use drugs are disproportionately likely to be arrested for, charged with, and convicted of a *drug felony* (Chasnoff, Landress, and Barrett 1990; Neuspiel 1996), their children are disproportionately likely to suffer the consequences. This set of bans has resulted in one of the most devastating effects of maternal incarceration on African American children: abandonment in the system of foster care and a failure to be reunited with their mothers.

In short, though all people face barriers to reentry after a period of incarceration, some barriers are uniquely "gendered and raced" (O'Brien 2001; Sokoloff 2003). As noted in our discussion above, while White and Hispanic children of prisoners generally live with relatives, African American children are disproportionately likely to be in foster care, making regaining custody significantly harder for African American mothers. As a result, African American children are unnecessarily likely to *age out* of foster care before their mothers are able to regain custody (Ross, Khashu, and Wamsley 2004).

Fortunately for Kezia, her children were placed with her mother while she was incarcerated. Secondly, her sentence was relatively short. As a result, at the time we interviewed her, all of Kezia's five children were living with her and she had managed, through a local church, to get a public housing authority official to lease her a public housing unit. Kezia has an uphill battle if she is going to make it and not end up in the unfortunately all-too-common revolving door of prison. Like some of the men we profiled in chapter 3, Kezia has several things working in her favor: she has reestablished her familial relationships with her children and with her mother, and thus she has access to support on the one hand and a sense of purpose on the other. Second, she is re-domiciled in an apartment she can afford. Third, though she was convicted of felony possession she is not using or addicted to drugs, as Nick was. Only time will tell, but her prospects for successful reentry are greater than many of the other people we interviewed. That said, Kezia and all mothers who have been incarcerated face an additional set of challenges: raising children who do not end up in prison.

The Intergenerational Cycle of Incarceration

Although it seems convenient to generalize the impact upon children of having parents in prison, the actual behavioral responses of children are shaped by factors that are unique to their situation, including the gender of the parent, the age at which the separation occurs, and the length and disruptiveness of the incarceration. The gender of the imprisoned parent is one significant factor that tends to affect how children will respond to incarceration. Regardless of the gender of the child, the response of children affected by *maternal incarceration* can be characterized as "acting in" behavior, such as crying and emotional withdrawal. *Paternal incarceration* generally provokes in children behavior characterized as "acting out," which includes truancy and running away (Fritsch and Burkhead 1981) or being the victims or perpetrators of violence (Prothrow-Stith and Weissman 1991). There is some speculation that children of incarcerated parents are more likely to use alcohol or drugs, become sexually active as teenagers, become teen parents, and fail to graduate high school than their counterparts. However, verifying these relationships statistically is difficult because as many researchers have documented (Petersilia 2003; Visher, LaVigne, and Travis 2004), the incarcerated population tends to be drawn from communities plagued by other risk factors for the above-mentioned problems including poverty, racial segregation, low levels of adult education, high unemployment, low-resourced schools, and so on. Nevertheless, we can assume that having an incarcerated parent intensifies the risks already present.

The age at which the parent-child separation occurs is a second factor that contributes to the response of children to incarceration. Generally separation is more harmful when the child is young. Unfortunately comprehensive findings to date, which have focused on the female prison population, indicate that almost two-thirds of children are younger than ten and nearly a quarter younger than four at the time of their mothers' incarceration (Mumola 2000). This finding is significant because it illustrates the fact that the majority of children experience separation from their mothers during their early formative years when a positive nurturing relationship is essential for healthy child development (McGowan and Blumenthal 1978).

The length and disruptiveness of the incarceration is a third predictive factor that tends to correlate with how a child will respond to having an imprisoned parent. In addition to lowering the likelihood of recidivism among incarcerated parents, there is evidence that maintaining contact with one's incarcerated parent improves a child's emotional response to the incarceration and supports parent-child attachment (La Vigne, Naser, Brooks, and Castro 2005). As noted previously, this is more difficult when the prison sentence is lengthy.

One of the most devastating outcomes of parental incarceration is the perpetuation of the intergenerational cycle of incarceration. Statistics from the U.S. Department of Justice show that children of offenders are six times more likely than their peers to be incarcerated, and one in ten will be confined before ever becoming an adult (Favro 2007). Interestingly, a 2004 Justice Department report indicated that nearly half of the then–two million offenders in state prisons reported having a relative who was or had been incarcerated (Bureau of Justice Statistics 2004). Within the juvenile justice system, more than half of the confined population has at least one parent who is or was in prison (Favro 2007). All of these numbers indicate that there is a strong correlation between family ties and crime.

Conclusions

We conclude this chapter by summarizing a few key points.

- Women, and African American women in particular, are the fastest-growing demographic group in prisons.
- Women are disproportionately likely to be incarcerated for drug possession. As we note in chapter 3 we recommend that drug policies focus more on treatment than on incarcerating drug users.
- The majority of women, nearly 90 percent who are incarcerated, are mothers of minor children and 60 percent of these mothers lived with their minor children immediately before incarceration.
- Children of incarcerated mothers are significantly less likely to live with their fathers and significantly more likely to live in foster care than children of incarcerated fathers. And, this is further exacerbated by race.

- As a result of adopting the "sameness" approach to incarcerating women, those who are pregnant and give birth during their term of incarceration (6 percent of all incarcerated women) are subjected to procedures that are ridiculous at best and violate their human rights at worst.
- Mothers face significant barriers to maintaining contact and custody of their minor children while they are incarcerated.
- There are pilot programs in several states that are attempting to keep mothers and their children highly connected during periods of incarceration. The hope is that this will reduce the negative consequences on both mothers and children.
- Reentry is a gendered and racialized experience. Mothers, particularly African American mothers, face significant barriers to becoming self-sufficient and to regaining custody of their children upon reentry. These processes are exacerbated by the welfare reforms of 1996 that prohibit those with felony drug convictions from accessing a set of critical safety-net programs including public housing and TANF.
- Children of incarcerated mothers are at significantly greater risk for engaging in drug and alcohol use and abuse, becoming sexually active, and being incarcerated themselves.

Women have always made up a very small proportion—about 10 percent—of the incarcerated population in the United States. Over the last two decades, however, in the wake of the drug reform laws enacted in the early 1980s, the number of women being incarcerated has risen dramatically. As a result state departments of corrections, local county sheriffs, and federal prison administrators have had to develop policies for dealing with the rise in women inmates.

In general, but lacking any required guidelines, the majority of jail and prison administrators have adopted a "sameness" strategy for dealing with women as inmates. As a result, for example, when incarcerated women are pregnant and ready to give birth—an experience that happens in the local hospital—they are treated as any other inmate would be with regards to transport. Laboring mothers are handcuffed to belly chains and shackled in leg irons while they are transported from their prison cells to the hospital. Once in the labor and delivery room, they labor and deliver while shackled and handcuffed to the bed rails. Their infants are immediately removed from them; the mothers are sent back to prison within hours and the infants, if not "claimed" within twenty-four hours, are put into foster care. These procedures and practices make an already-difficult experience—

labor and delivery—unnecessarily more difficult and furthermore they expose the mothers and their infants to greater risks for medical complications.

Incarcerated mothers face enormous barriers to mothering including distance, rules for contact visits, and the irregularity of their own movement. As a result, many lose legal custody of their children as a result of the Adoption and Safe Families Act. When they are released from prison, and most are, they face enormous barriers to reestablishing family connections and often have significant challenges to regaining custody of their children. This process is exacerbated by the fact that the welfare reform of 1996 bans access to virtually all safety-net programs to those with drug felony convictions. Thus, the process of reestablishing self-sufficiency is unnecessarily difficult.

Finally, the children of incarcerated mothers, and there are approximately 1.5 million, are at significantly higher risk for a host of problems including teen pregnancy, early sexual activity, drug and alcohol use and abuse, dropping out of high school, and their own incarceration as juveniles and adults.

Perhaps most problematic is that a large percentage (63 percent) of mothers who are incarcerated were convicted for nonviolent property crimes and/or drug possession (Mumola 2000). We advocate the implementation of alternatives to incarceration in cases such as these. As we stated emphatically in chapter 3, drug users need treatment, not incarceration. This is of particular importance because very little drug treatment happens in prison. Many women who are convicted of nonviolent property crimes such as stealing and writing bad checks are stuck in a cycle of poverty. Implementing laws that pay living wages to all Americans and legislating and enforcing the equal pay act would reduce the number of women who are forced to engage in these types of crimes as a way to feed their children (Edin and Lein 1997). Lastly, as pointed out earlier, these same women are often committing these property crimes as part of an exit strategy as they leave violent homes and partners. Providing support for battered women and their children would also greatly reduce the number of women incarcerated for these types of crimes.

It is a tragedy when a mother goes to prison. It is a double tragedy when a child is left behind. We advocate strongly for programs outlined above that are designed to reduce the negative impact of incarceration on both mothers and children. These programs offer a glimmer of hope for breaking the intergenerational cycle of incarceration. In the next chapter we focus specifically on the role of social capital in the process of reentry.

Notes

1. www.ojp.usdoj.gov/bjs/crimoff.htm#women.

2. Bureau of Justice Statistics, www.ojp.usdoj.gov/bjs/pub/pdf/cpus98.pdf.

3. More recently debates have erupted over laws that would charge mothers who deliver drug-addicted babies with child abuse, neglect, child endangerment, and even murder if the child subsequently dies.

4. www.childtrendsdatabank.org/figures/12-Figure-2.gif.

5. B. E. Richie, (2001), "Challenges Incarcerated Women Face as They Return to Their Communities: Findings from Life History Interviews," *Crime and Delinquency* 47:368–89.

6. Prisons have no requirement to alert family members that an inmate has been transferred. Thus, unless the inmate has a chance to place a telephone call or the transfer is arranged well in advance—which is not typical—and he or she can send a letter, often family members arrive for visits only to be told that their loved one is now incarcerated in another facility.

6

The Impact of Social Capital on Reentry

Just as a screwdriver (physical capital) or a college education (human capital) can increase productivity (both individual and collective), so do social contacts affect the productivity of individuals and groups. (Putnam 2000:18–19)

IN THE PREVIOUS CHAPTERS, especially chapters 3, 4, and 5, we chronicled the long road home that reentry felons face. Critical to their success are several core issues, especially stable housing and employment. As noted in chapter 2, reentry felons, especially those with drug felonies, face enormous barriers to securing both of these key elements. And, though many of the men we interviewed set up their own barriers to reentry, for example by not seeking treatment for an addiction, the barriers to reentry are largely controlled by the government (e.g., bans on social welfare) and by the beliefs and prejudices that employers and rental agencies hold about individuals who have been to prison. And, though the situation may seem hopeless, especially after reading the cases of individuals like Eddie and Nick, our interviews revealed that one avenue for hope is providing reentry felons with access to social capital and social networks that can serve to open doors of opportunity—especially with regards to housing and employment—that would otherwise be closed. In this chapter we focus on the role that social capital can play in the reentry experience.

What Is Social Capital?

The concept of "capital" is generally understood to be a set of resources that individuals (or institutions) access in order to have agency in a market. Karl Marx (2005) wrote about capital in terms of one's relationship to "the means of production." Specifically Marx conceptualized capital as the resources that are necessary to produce commodities for the market: land that was necessary to grow and produce food, natural resources such as taconite or coal mines, and the machinery necessary to transform resources into commodities. "Neo-capitalists," as Lin (2000) refers to them, used Marx's concept of capital and expanded it in order to analyze the kinds of resources that individuals hold inside themselves, such as education or training (human capital), or among their social networks (social capital). Specific to our argument here, Lin argues:

> Social capital may be defined as investment and use of embedded resources in social relations for expected returns. Social capital is conceptualized as (1) quantity and/or quality of resources that an actor (be it an individual or group or community) can access or use through (2) its location in a social network. (Lin 2000:786)

In other words, there are two key aspects to social capital: social networks and the resources that are embedded within these social networks that an actor can access. Breaking it down even further, for readers who may be unfamiliar with this concept, social networks are comprised of the people with whom one has sufficient relations to be able to ask advice or seek assistance. Social capital theorists often distinguish between what they refer to as "strong ties" and "weak ties." Perhaps counterintuitive, it is better to have social networks comprised of many weak ties than those comprised of just a few strong ties. Strong ties are those relationships we have that are very close: with parents, spouse/partners, other relatives, long-time friends, and so forth. Weak ties can be thought of more in terms of acquaintances: the other parents we see at our children's weekly soccer games, colleagues at work—especially those with whom we rarely socialize—members of our congregation or temple, and so forth.

Why would social capital theorists argue that social networks built on weak ties are better than those built on strong ties? Primarily because of the principle of homophily, or the tendency we have to build our strongest relationships with people whom we are the most like. The majority of Americans spend most of their time in social groups that are homogenous with regards to key variables such as race, religion, and especially educational background and social class. Thus, social networks based on strong ties will tend to be homogenous. If one's social networks are incredibly resource rich, then this may not be so problematic, but for the most part scholars of social capital agree that the best returns on social capital occur when social networks are diverse and thus the types of resources embedded in the network are also diverse.

What are the types of resources that are embedded in social networks? Primarily the resources to which theorists analyzing social capital are referring revolve around information and the ability to refer. For example, a social network that is resource rich will typically include people who have access to information about jobs, or better yet the ability to refer an individual directly to the person in charge of hiring, or better still, the ability to hire! Similarly, the types of resources that constitute social capital also include information or the ability to refer or better yet the ability to influence the admissions process at a prestigious institution of hiring learning.[1] Thus, the more resource rich one's social capital network, the more access one has to opportunities related to education, employment, running for political office, and so forth.

Why does diversity matter? Diversity in social networks matters primarily because very few individuals possess information, the ability to refer, or the ability to influence outcomes—such as hiring or admission—that extends beyond more than one area—education *or* employment—or beyond more than one or two institutions. For example, the authors' ability to provide information about higher education is relatively high, but either of our abilities to provide a *strong* referral are limited to a few institutions at which we have previously worked or studied or where we have colleagues who work. Thus, a student seeking to attend graduate school would be best served by having "weak" relationships with many faculty members rather than a network built on "strong" ties with only a few faculty.

Perhaps this is best illustrated when we think about running for political office, be it at the local, state, or national level. Because many votes must be garnered in order to win an election, a candidate with a very diverse social network built on weak ties will be able to mobilize many more votes than a candidate with a very homogenous social network built on very strong relationships with a few individuals. Certainly the support of key individuals is important—that's why candidates seek endorsements from powerful people—but the key to winning is mobilizing thousands or even millions of people one has never met to go to the polls and vote.

Social Capital and Inequality

Of course, not everyone has access to the same types of social networks and thus not everyone has access to the same social capital resources. As Lin

(2000) demonstrates, social capital and social networks (1) vary by social location and (2) produce and reproduce existing social inequalities. For example, research on social capital and gender note that women have less access to diverse social networks and their networks tend to be poorer in resources than are men's. Scholars of gender and social capital (Green, Leann, Tigges, and Browne 1995; Hanson and Pratt 1991) generally attribute this to the public/private split that arose during the industrial revolution and relegated women to the work of the home (the private sphere) and men to the paid labor market (the public sphere) (Padavic and Reskin 2002). The resultant sex segregation in the work place, which has persisted despite the fact that currently nearly half of all paid employees are women (Padavic and Reskin 2002), structures the types of social networks that men and women have access to and thus contributes to the persistence of gender inequality, particularly that associated with employment and pay.

Similarly, as Portes and others (Portes 1998; Portes and Stepnick 1985; Wilson and Portes 1980) have documented, access to social capital also varies tremendously, and in the expected direction, by race and ethnicity. Overall, Whites have the most access to social capital and the most diverse and resource-rich social networks, African Americans have the least access and the "poorest" networks, and Hispanics and Asians fall in the middle. As with gender, the history of racial segregation that has persisted throughout U.S. history plays a crucial role in structuring differential access to social networks and the social capital embedded in these networks. As Lin (2000) argues, people have a tendency toward "homophily" or the desire to associate mostly with people like themselves. Additionally, the severe and intentional segregation that has persisted with regards to housing, education, and religious practices is perhaps more important in producing social networks that are largely racially homogenous. Either way, these differences in access to social networks, and the resources embedded in these networks, produce and reproduce racial inequality.

Social Class

Though Lin (2000) begins with a brief summary of the development of the term "social capital" by neo-capital theorists, he does not return to a discussion of class as a status with regards to differential access to social capital; rather he deals with social class only as an *outcome* of social capital. Yet, we believe that class can be both a status and an outcome and thus it is worth following the logical path and examining its power to segregate or be segregated and thus shape access to social capital and social networks.

We argue that, as is the case with both gender and race, social class as a status significantly shapes access to social networks and social capital that thus produce and reproduce class status. For example, just as housing is segregated by race/ethnicity, it is also segregated by social class, especially for Whites, but also for members of other racial/ethnic groups. Driving through any community illustrates this point. Zoning laws shape the social class make-up of neighborhoods by either preventing or encouraging multiple family dwellings, for example, or by requiring that homes be of a certain minimum size. As a result, it is very uncommon for neighborhoods to be socioeconomically "mixed." This in and of itself shapes individual's access to social networks and social capital. Furthermore, because the neighborhood an individual lives in dictates things like the schools his or her children will attend, the access high- and low-income children have to social networks and social capital will be highly shaped by their social class alone and in combination with their access to the social capital resources embedded in particular school settings.

Secondly, though occupations employ people of all social classes, both structures and norms severely limit interactions among people who occupy different locations in the occupational hierarchy. Professionals of any type— physicians, lawyers, accountants; investors, even college professors—rarely interact with staff who clean our bathrooms and offices or who groom the grounds on which we work. Certainly there are many professionals who have hallway "chats" with the specific person who cleans their office, for example, but these interactions rarely if ever leave the workplace nor do they often extend beyond the two individuals to include the entire janitorial staff, for example, or either person's family. Thus, one's social class determines one's position in the occupational hierarchy, which in turn determines the physical location of one's work and ultimately his or her access to social networks and social capital. Finally, we should note that because of the ways that systems of inequality are interwoven, there will be significant variation inside each system based on one's other identities. For example, women of color will experience a higher level of exclusion from social networks and social capital than White women, and poor women of all races will experience more exclusion than their wealthy and/or professional counterparts. Thus, the interlocking systems of inequality and privilege will further shape the likelihood that an individual can access heterogeneous social networks that are rich in social capital.

Principle of Exclusion

Clearly then institutionalized segregation such as occurs in occupations (the workplace), housing, education, worship, and any other institution shapes the core elements Lin (2000) argues are central to social capital: (1) social networks and (2) the social capital embedded in these networks. Because reentry felons are predominately members of racial and ethnic minorities—African Americans and Hispanics—who have been subjected historically to high levels of institutionalized segregation and because they are predominately from low-income backgrounds, another "group" that is highly segregated, they are likely to have limited social networks that are resource poor. That said, based on the work of (Murray 2007) we argue here that an additional process—exclusion—produces outcomes similar to institutionalized segregation.

The principle of exclusion focuses on the way in which certain statuses exclude individuals with that status from participation in mainstream life (Foster and Hagan 2009) and they argue further that this exclusion often extends to the excluded individual's family members as well. Scholars who study status note that there are certain statuses that trump all other statuses—referred to as "master statuses"—and that cling to an individual's identity for his or her entire life. Examples of master status include being handicapped—particularly if the disability is readily apparent such as having lost a limb or being blind—suffering from mental illness or a chronic disease—again especially if it is readily apparent such as suffering from a seizure syndrome such as epilepsy. The status of inmate or prisoner, even when it is preceded by "ex" is a prime example of a master status. Not only is it symbolically attached to an individual for the remainder of their lifetime, but also this particular status is reinforced by laws such as Megan's Law, which requires a convicted sex offender to register and regularly update his (or her) contact information in both a book that his kept at the county sheriff's department and also an electronic database that is available to the public and "searchable."

More generally, all individuals with a felony record feel this master status because of employment laws that require job applicants to disclose that they have a felony and requirements inside the TANF laws that demand disclosure of a felony so that services can be denied. These legal measures *reinforce* the master status, especially for sex offenders and those with felony convictions, in a manner that is unique compared to the other types of master statuses we noted above. Furthermore, the legal reinforcement of these statues further cements them to an individual's identity.

Separate from a reentry felon's segregated existence due to race/ethnicity and/or social class, their master status as a felon or sex offender operates similarly through the principle of exclusion. Individuals with felony convictions and/or sex offender convictions are excluded—both formally and informally—from many aspects of social life. For example, as noted throughout this book, drug felons and sex offenders are banned for their lifetime from living in public housing. This ban creates a form of exclusion that denies them access to certain social networks and the consequent resources. For example, scholars of employment note that the most likely pathway to a job is through social contacts or networks—what we colloquially referred to as "word of mouth." Though residents of public housing are unlikely to have social contacts or social networks that include employers looking to hire, they are capable of bringing home news that the boss at their job is hiring. By excluding drug felons and sex offenders from the social networks in public housing they are denied access to valuable social capital—in this case information about a job—that are embedded in these social networks. This type of exclusion is formal, but there are other forms of exclusion that are informal yet create the same type of marginalization and disadvantage. For example, frequently one who watches the news or reads the newspaper will learn of a community in which a sex offender is denied the right to purchase a home or rent an apartment. Though sex offenders may not be legally banned from living in certain neighborhoods as long as the potential housing they are considering doesn't violate the other limitations placed on sex offenders, because they are required to register and in some cases to notify their potential neighbors when they are moving in, neighbors may band together and ostracize the individual to the point that he (or she) feels so unwelcome that they decide not to move in to their potential new home. This type of informal exclusion is very powerful in shaping the housing patterns of sex offenders. And, similar to de jure or de facto housing segregation, this process of exclusion will ultimately limit the types of social networks that sex offenders will have access to vis-à-vis their neighborhood and thus limit their access to social capital.

A similar process occurs with regards to education: both formal and informal mechanisms of exclusion significantly shape felons' access to social capital. Formally, there are certain occupations that felons and/or sex offenders may not hold, including being a certified barber or tattoo artist (Mukamal 2004) or, in the case of sex offenders, any job that is near any number of locations where children are present—including working as a janitorial staff in a school. As is the case with the way in which occupational sex segregation limits the social networks and access to social capital for women, formal exclusion from occupations results in a similar limitation for felons. Informally, employers who work in occupations or occupational settings that do not ban felons or sex offenders are not legally obligated to hire a felon or sex offender: they can *legally discriminate.* Thus, as we heard over and over and over from the men and women we interviewed, the process of disclosing their status as a felon was, at least in their minds, the *key factor that prevented them from obtaining employment.* Again, just as was the case with housing, the principle of exclusion as it operates in employment severely restricts a reentry felon's access to networks and social capital. We turn now to the stories we heard from the men we interviewed about their own access to social networks and how this access translated (or not) into employment and housing.

Social Capital, the Principle of Exclusion and the Reentry Felon

So, how does the theory we have reviewed and developed in this chapter thus far translate into real outcomes for reentry felons? What kinds of social networks do reentry felons have access to and do they help or hurt the reentry felon with regards to his or her attempts at reentry? We will explore these questions through the lens provided by men and women we interviewed.

Family and Friends

As most readers already know, no matter how much an individual has hurt his or her family, most inmates report that their greatest access to contact with the "free world" is through their families. And, even inside of this broad category, for male inmates it is their mothers and their female partners who provide the most contact—visits, letters, phone calls—and emotional support. For female inmates it is often just their own mothers who consistently write and visit them and provide support. (The reader will recall the discussion in chapter 5 of women's experiences in prison.) Thus, upon release, it is this very small social network, based on very strong ties, to which an inmate returns. As noted in chapter 3, we interviewed many former drug dealers who, upon their release, moved back in with their mothers! Adult men, who had once strolled the streets with pockets of cash, were reduced to relying on the only social support they had—their mothers—for their survival.

Relying on social capital theory as a way of analyzing the experiences reentry felons face when they return to the "free world," it becomes immediately clear that one barrier they face to successful reentry is a lack of social capital. As a result of their behavior prior to incarceration as well as the stresses of incarceration itself, the majority of reentry felons have burned many bridges and their social networks have shrunk to just a few people with whom they have had long and intimate relationships—immediate family members. These social networks are obviously very narrow and lack the diversity of contacts that Lin (2000) and others claim improves the likelihood of accessing important resources. Additionally, as noted above, most inmates come from communities on the margin: they are typically racial/ethnic minorities from low-income backgrounds. Thus, the few ties they have in their social networks are not likely to have access to the kinds of information and power that produce resources that will enhance one's ability to find housing or employment or gain access to further education. Thus, the inmate is doubly disadvantaged: he or she is disadvantaged based on his or her location in the social hierarchy and within that location his or her period of incarceration is likely to shrink the little social capital that existed prior to incarceration.

Though Llee's circumstances of having to live with his mother are dismal, what is even worse is when an inmate has burned *all* of his or her bridges—as was the case with both of the sex offenders we profiled in chapter 4, Brandon and Eddie—and is released from prison to a homeless shelter. Though a homeless shelter population will certainly produce a social network based on weak ties, the population itself is so homogenous and the resources each individual has are so extremely limited that there is very little useable social capital that can be derived from a social capital network built on homeless shelter residents. Thus, the individuals released to a family member or spouse/partner—as resource poor as these social networks are—are clearly at an advantage over those released to a homeless shelter.

Homeless Shelters and Reentry

As we noted in chapter 3, for a significant subpopulation of reentry felons, a cycle develops between two marginalized institutions: prison and homeless shelters. As noted above, one aspect of reentry that differentiates ex-inmates from most other populations is their master status, which leads to their exclusion from much of mainstream society. The majority of Americans have probably never been inside a prison and though slightly more have probably been to a homeless shelter as part of a volunteer project, most Americans know very little about either of these institutions. And, though they are clearly very different institutions, they share much in common, not the least of which is their isolation from mainstream culture and, for the purposes of this discussion, social capital networks. Homeless shelters, like prisons, are structured such that individuals living there have very little personal choice: they eat what is served, they sleep where there is an open cot, and they wake each morning when the shelter director tells them to—usually around 5:30 or 6 am. Shelter residents have to abide by numerous rules, such as a curfew—most shelters require residents to be inside by dinner time and they are not allowed to leave once they arrive each evening—most shelters require residents to vacate the property during the entire day—typically from 7 am until 7 pm—most require sobriety, they severely limit the number of personal items that can be stored, and they often have rules such as at our local homeless shelter where men are not allowed to have more than two cigarettes in their possession at one time. As our students report after volunteering overnight at the shelter, they find it humiliating that grown men must ask them—teenagers and young adults—to dispense no more than the allotted number of cigarettes from their individual packs, which they are required to leave behind a counter where they can be monitored by a volunteer. Finally, most shelters offer no personal privacy—residents sleep dormitory style and use dormitory or "gang" type showers and toilets. The authors were both struck upon analyzing the interviews that homeless shelters share much in common with prisons.

Thus, part of the struggle that many reentry felons face is that they are "trapped" in institutions that are marginalized and kept far away from mainstream society. Additionally, and we observe this frequently when we visit the shelter, perhaps because shelters resemble prisons or perhaps because so many of the residents have been incarcerated, norms of behavior and interaction look very similar in and around the shelter as they do inside a prison and especially in the "yard." Working with reentry felons and spending time observing them, it is painfully obvious that they carry norms and the prison "culture" with them when they exit prison. Reentry felons, especially those who have been released relatively recently, might as well have their master status tattooed on their foreheads because their behavior reveals their status so apparently. What do we mean? Reentry felons often pace, sometimes they stand, at a doorway or on the curb at an intersection, almost as if they are waiting for someone to tell them when to walk and where to go. Inmates quickly develop an ability to observe what is going on around them—this is necessary in order to avoid being shanked or blind-sided by a punch or raped—and they carry this habit back in to the "free world" such that they appear as if their heads are on swivels. Many reentry felons retain the habit of looking down and not looking another person directly in the eyes. The list goes on and on. And, for those who cycle back to homeless shelters, where they are surrounded by other reentry felons in a structure so similar to prison with little privacy and reason to fear, these habits not only don't die, but are also reinforced and embedded more deeply into a reentry felon's mannerisms. This is yet another negative, though perhaps unintended, consequence of the principle of exclusion that has potentially significant consequences for those attempting to rebuild their lives, find employment, and reestablish relationships.

In addition to being physically excluded from mainstream culture—most homeless shelters, like prisons, are not within walking distance of the local mall or movie theaters or any of the other institutions we take for granted—the population at homeless shelters is about as resource poor as possible. Thus, a social network populated primarily by residents of a homeless shelter is not likely to provide access to the types of resources that Lin (2000:786) describes as being likely to produce "instrumental returns, such as better jobs, earlier promotions, higher earnings or bonuses, and expressive returns such as better mental health." What we have observed among the reentry felons whom we have interviewed and with whom we have worked is that the homeless shelter social network is primarily valuable in providing information (resources) about which church runs the best soup kitchen or which organizations can be approached for other types of handouts such as clothing or bus passes. Certainly a small percentage of homeless shelter residents are employed and they might be able to pass on information about hiring that is being done at their current job, but they lack the social and political capital to serve as a reference or influence the hiring process. Furthermore, the types of jobs about which they have knowledge are typically the lowest paid, most undesirable jobs in the local economy. And clearly, if they had information (resources) about housing they wouldn't be homeless themselves! Thus, whether it be the exclusion that results from the physical marginalization of the homeless shelter or the exclusion from resource-rich social networks that homeless shelter residents experience, reentry felons, like Nick, who are released from prison directly to a homeless shelter are likely to cycle back to prison in part because the homeless shelter and its residents are excluded from mainstream culture and from key social capital resources, especially those related to employment and housing, which are the critical elements to successful reentry.

Hanging Out in the Neighborhood/Gang Bangers

Of course, not all social networks and social capital are contained within mainstream culture. Historically we have many studies that demonstrate the role that networks in the illegitimate economy can play in providing access to social capital. In organizations such as the mafia or in gangs that populate our major cities today—the Crips, the Bloods, and so forth—social networks embedded in the illegitimate economy can and do provide resource-rich social capital, and can provide the types of "returns" Lin (2000) describes: housing, "employment," "promotion," and even safety. Of course because these social networks exist outside of the mainstream and they rely primarily on illegitimate activities in order to generate income and wealth, the likelihood that one will successfully reenter and not recidivate is low if one chooses to rely on this type of social network for his or her social capital. A majority of the men we interviewed who had cycled in and out of prison, often for more than two decades, recounted a lifetime of these choices. Many, including William and Kevin, and so many others, recalled that after their first or second or tenth prison sentence was served they returned to their home community with a vow to stay straight and get their lives turned around. For some, the return to drug dealing was immediate: they knew nothing else. For others, they made sincere attempts to "go straight" but, unable to find employment and generate enough income to take care of themselves, pay child support, and so forth, they returned to "hustling" out of frustration and in order to survive. As Kevin said (we paraphrase), "Why would I labor all day at a job that pays minimum wage when I can pick up a few rocks (crack-cocaine), walk around the block a few times, and turn $100 profit?" Or for men like Brandon and Eddie who are released to a homeless shelter, as noted not exactly rich in social capital, they may find they have no other option than to return to their former friends or associates and engage in hustling in order to survive. Clearly, then, gangs or "associations" are interesting because they do provide social capital, but the resources embedded in these social networks—rich as they may seem—are so far removed from the mainstream that they typically require a return to illegitimate or criminal activity and more than likely a return to prison.

Alternative Social Networks

As the reader will recall from the discussion in chapter 2, Devah Pager's (2003) study demonstrated that men with a felony record face serious barriers to employment and that the impact is significantly intensified for African American men with felony convictions. Thus, one of the issues we wanted to explore in our interviews with reentry felons was their experience with seeking and obtaining employment. As we noted in chapter 2, the majority of men reported that job seeking was both frustrating and unfruitful. The majority had not been able to secure a job since they were released from prison. But perhaps more devastating were the lessons they learned that reinforced Pager's findings. Some men reported, for example, that they were initially hired, but once the employer ran the background check (usually within the first thirty days but no later than ninety days after the commencement of employment) and their criminal record was disclosed, they were fired. Others reported that an otherwise enthusiastic interview turned suddenly cold when they revealed that the certificates they had earned in welding, electrical, and other construction trades were earned at a correctional facility. After conducting several interviews that told this story we wondered if there were any stories of hope.

Early on, we got our first indication that social capital might be an important factor when Tito revealed that after several stints of incarceration—primarily for possession of drugs and dealing drugs in Miami, Florida—he was able to find employment through family members and friends who owned small businesses. He was certain that his current bout of unemployment was not primarily a result of his long criminal record but was due to the fact that in order to escape the gang influences in Miami he had moved to rural North Carolina to live with his mother. He assumed that the fact that he didn't know anyone here was the primary reason he couldn't get a job. Without knowing it, Tito was giving us our first clue about the importance of social capital in the reentry experiences of felons.

As we interviewed more and more people the story that emerged got more and more complicated until it culminated in the last interview we conducted, which happened to be with Mr. Lyman Sykes. As the reader will recall, we introduced Lyman in chapter 3 in order to illustrate the impact of addiction and getting clean on an individual's trajectory. We return to Lyman's story here in order to examine and illustrate the role that alternative forms of social capital can play in reentry.

As the reader will recall, when we met Lyman he was in his early sixties and he had spent a total of nearly thirty-five years in prison, primarily for property crimes that he committed as part of his heroin addiction. One of the most interesting and compelling aspects of Lyman's life is that following his last stint in prison he was able to do something the majority of men we interviewed were unable to do: get a job and keep it. Curious about Lyman's experience because it was so unique, we questioned him at length. Lyman described his exit from prison, some two years before our interview. He had met Darryl Hunt while they were both incarcerated (the reader will become very well-acquainted with Mr. Hunt in the next chapter). He and Darryl became friends. Several years before Lyman's release from prison Darryl was released—he was exonerated for a rape and murder he did not commit—and shortly after his exoneration, determined to contribute to the community that stood by him, Darryl established a nonprofit organization focused on prisoner reentry. Immediately upon being released, Lyman sought out Darryl. The reader will recall that Lyman was also fortunate in that his wife stood by him during all of his periods of incarceration such that, unlike Nick or Brandon or Eddie, he moved back home with her rather than into a homeless shelter. Seeing some potential in Lyman, Darryl made a commitment to personally help Lyman with the battles a reentry felon with a long list of drug felony convictions faces. Darryl drew on his own political capital and he brokered a job for Lyman at a local Church's Chicken—a low-level fast food restaurant that is popular in the south, especially in low-income communities. The manager gave Lyman a chance. Lyman's smile lit his whole face when he talked about the pride he felt getting his first job in the legitimate economy at the ripe old age of sixty! Since he was initially hired, Lyman has been promoted to assistant manager and he has been steadily employed for the past three years. William, whose story we also presented in chapter 3, is also employed. Though he served much less time in prison, he is the typical person Pager's (2003) study identified as least likely to get a job: an African American man with a drug felony conviction. Like Lyman, he was hired after Darryl leveraged a personal relationship: he knows the owner of a local restaurant who agreed, based on Darryl's reference, to give William a chance. Most recently, in talking with some reentry felons who participate in the Darryl Hunt Project for Freedom and Justice

"Homecoming" program, they revealed that Darryl has leveraged some personal relationship he has with the city and as a result the city department of sanitation and transportation has agreed to hire some of the reentry felons Darryl refers.

How Does this Muddy Findings Such as Pager's?

One of the most interesting aspects of doing social science research involving interviews with real people is that often their experiences are contradictory to the reigning theory and scientific literature. These cases are perplexing and force us to go beyond what we currently hold to be true and seek alternative ways of explaining the phenomena. This was certainly the case when we conducted these interviews. Though our sample size is small enough that statistics are inappropriate, general patterns are revealing. For our purposes here, we note that none of the White men we interviewed (ten) were employed following their most recent period of incarceration but three (of twelve) of the African American men were. These findings run entirely counter to what all of the literature, including Pager's (2003) landmark study, reveals about the intersection of race, incarceration, and employment. As we worked to make sense of the data, it was immediately apparent that one of the key differences between the experiences of the men who were employed and those who were not was their access to the personal resources of a single man: Darryl Hunt.[2]

Thus we began to ask the question, can a reentry program, and in particular a staff member of that reentry program, provide a surrogate social network that is embedded with enough social capital resources to overcome the double trap that the African American men with drug convictions in Pager's study experienced? In observing and working with Darryl Hunt, the answer seems to be, cautiously, "yes." Though the reentry program is built primarily around one person, Mr. Hunt, and some supporting staff, and though this hardly constitutes the diverse social network that Lin (2000) proclaims enhances an individual's returns on their investment, for men who experience the highest levels of exclusion and who have access to very little social capital outside of the reentry program, the resources embedded in the reentry social network appear to be the best chance they have for successful reentry. Clearly, as noted in the accompanying footnote, other things must be in place as well: the men must be free from addiction and it is useful if they have other social relationships that help them to meet other needs that they have for housing and/or intimacy. Additionally, as with any individual accessing a social network, the reentry felon must convince the individual with the social capital (Darryl Hunt) that they are worthy of the investment. And, perhaps the success we saw in these men was in part a result of selection bias—Mr. Hunt is only willing to broker for men he truly believes have the potential for success. Yet, these findings suggest that in addition to those factors (race and felony status) that Pager identifies, *social capital may be one of the most important factors in prisoner reentry.*

This would certainly explain why most white-collar criminals are able to reenter successfully—in addition to the human capital they retain they also retain social capital. This may explain why social organizations like the mafia or gangs are able to provide help with reentry—that is until the individual is caught again participating in illegal activity, arrested, and recidivated. What all of these cases share in common is access to social networks that are rich enough in resources to provide the kind of social capital that is necessary to secure employment and stable housing: the two critical elements in successful reentry.

What Does All of This Mean?

What all of this means is that for those of us concerned about extremely high recidivism rates and the barriers to successful reentry, we should work to develop and invest in programs and people that can create and provide the kinds of social capital that can be accessed by reentry felons: men and women who are otherwise excluded from mainstream society as a whole and viable social networks in particular. Reentry felons have a lot of work to do to be accountable for their previous behavior, for beating addictions, and for making amends in their personal lives. But, for those who do, reentry programs like the Darryl Hunt Project for Freedom and Justice and so many others that are housed in church ministries or run by ex-inmates who have successfully reentered the "free world" themselves may be a viable source of social capital that can assist reentry felons in successfully beating the cycle of incarceration. We urge other scholars as well as those interested in public policy and public safety to turn their attention toward rigorous and detailed examination of this potential source of social capital for reentry felons. Lastly, we suggest that it is in all our best interest to identify and seek mechanisms that ease reentry for as a matter of public safety we all benefit when recidivism rates are low and those who have made mistakes return to our communities better positioned to contribute as citizens rather than victimize us and consume the resources of our local criminal justice system.

Notes

1. At the time of the writing of this book, Henry Louis "Skip" Gates, Harvard University professor, was arrested for disorderly conduct when he was questioned about breaking into his own home. At a "beer summit" held by President Barack Obama, Gates offered to "help" the officer who arrested him "get his kids into Harvard." That's the ultimate in resource-rich social capital!

2. The men who were employed were also different in that they maintained relationships with female partners while they were incarcerated and none were living in a homeless shelter, though one man was living in a pre-release halfway house. Although all had been convicted of selling drugs, all three had beaten the addiction before they were released for the last time. Finally, none were convicted sex offenders. However, it is important to point out that there were plenty of White men who met these criterion as well.

7

The Special Case of Exonerees

I always said I was innocent, the question has always been was anybody listening

—Darryl Hunt[1]

IMAGINE THAT YOU ARE EIGHTEEN OR NINETEEN YEARS OLD and you have your whole life ahead of you. You have a passion that you think you can translate into a paycheck; maybe you already have your eye on a potential person you think you could settle down with and make a family; maybe you are simply enjoying the freedom that so many of us enjoy in those short years between adolescence and adulthood. Imagine that in the blink of an eye all of your dreams and hopes come crashing down on top of you. Imagine that your worst nightmare has come true. Imagine that you are not only arrested but also convicted of a crime you didn't commit. Imagine that you sit before a jury being called the mostly filthy and vile names—rapist, murderer—because the crime you are accused of is heinous. Imagine that you believed, you were taught, that the laws that give rights to defendants are there to prevent what is happening before your eyes. Imagine that you stand before a judge who sentences you to spend the rest of your life in prison, or worse, to stand in line to be executed. If you are one of the nearly 260 men and women who have been exonerated at the time of the writing of this book you don't have to imagine. This is what happened to you.

Exoneration: Some Definitions

To the general reader, the distinctions among terms such as exoneration, receiving a pardon, and commuting a sentence may seem unimportant because at the end of the day they all result in a similar outcome: an individual is released from their sentence. Yet, the distinctions among these terms are critically important because they illuminate problems that exist in the criminal justice system itself and unique barriers to individuals trying to reenter the "free world" after undergoing each of these processes. Thus, we begin with some basic definitions.

A *pardon* is the forgiveness of a crime and the penalty associated with it. It is granted by a head of state, such as a monarch or president, or by a competent church authority. A person receiving a pardon continues to admit they were guilty of the crime for which they were convicted. A pardon has nothing to do with being innocent. After he assumed the Presidency of the United States, Gerald Ford pardoned Richard Nixon for his role in the Watergate Scandal. *Clemency* is an associated term, meaning the lessening of the penalty of the crime without forgiving the crime itself. The act of clemency is a reprieve. Today, pardons and reprieves are granted in many countries when individuals have demonstrated that they have fulfilled their debt to society, or are otherwise deserving (in the opinion of the pardoning official) of a pardon or reprieve. *Commutation of sentence* involves the reduction of legal penalties, especially in terms of imprisonment. Unlike a pardon, a commutation does not nullify the conviction and is often conditional. In the United States, reduction of a sentence is handled by an executive head of government and is normally linked to prisoners' good behavior. The President of the United States solely holds the power to commute federal sentences while commutations of state charges are handled by the governor's office. A common use of commutation in the last decade has been for death row inmates. For example, if a state legislature or supreme court overturns the death penalty for that state, inmates on death row typically have their sentences commuted to life in prison.

In contrast, *exoneration* occurs when a person who has been convicted of a crime is later proved to have been *innocent* of that crime. Attempts to exonerate convicts are particularly controversial in death penalty cases, especially where new evidence is put forth after the execution has taken place. Exoneration, then, is reserved for those people who were "factually innocent" but who despite their actual innocence were wrongly convicted of a crime and served time in prison. Though exonerations can occur for a variety of reasons, including a witness recanting testimony or confessing to the crime, exonerations most frequently occur through the use of DNA analysis or reanalysis—using more sophisticated methods.

Exoneration: Some Statistics

Among the most recent phenomenon in the areas of crime and the law is the use of scientific forensic evidence—primarily DNA—to exonerate individuals who were wrongly convicted and incarcerated (Gross 2008; National Academy of Sciences 2009). At the time of the writing of this book, there were 251 exonerees. This is a number that is constantly in a state of flux as more and more individuals are granted the tools and the opportunity to gain their freedom. Thus, for the interested reader we recommend monitoring the website for The Innocence Project[2] for the most up-to-date count of exonerations.[3]

Scientifically speaking we don't know how many people there are sitting in our jails and prisons who are factually innocent. There is no systematic way of gaining an exoneration. Typically exonerations result from the dedicated work of attorneys like Mark Rabil who believe their client is innocent, investigative journalists who pay attention to serious inconsistencies in the evidence—as in the case of both Darryl Hunt and Roy Brown —and often the inmates themselves, like Ronald Cotton, who do their own detective and legal work trying to prove their innocence. Many, but not all, of these cases finally catch the attention of The Innocence Project, whose mission is to find and free wrongly convicted innocent people who rot for decades in American prisons.

Because the cases are handled on an individual basis, it is hard to estimate, but some experts suggest as much as 6 percent of our incarcerated population is actually innocent (Gross 2008). If that statistic is accurate, of the 2.2 million people who are currently incarcerated as many as 140,000 may be factually innocent.

Exoneration: The Human Costs

Wrongful conviction has in many regards claimed the lives of the 251 men and women who have been wrongly incarcerated. The average exonoree served twelve years in prison. The Innocence Project estimates that nearly 3,000 years have been collectively served by these 251 men and women, including the seventeen exonerees who served time on death row.

These years are, by all accounts, the best years of one's life. The average age at which the exonerees were incarcerated is twenty-six years old, but many were sent to prison for life while they were still in their late teens or early twenties. These are the years in which most Americans build their adult lives; they finish their education, they start working in their professions or occupations, they find life partners, they begin childbearing if they so choose, those with resources buy their first home, and so on. By and large the 251 men and women who have been exonerated spent most or all of these critical years in prison. Most of the exonerees had not married or otherwise entered committed relations, most had not started families, and most had not bought their own homes. Some had started their professional lives, but many had not. Regardless of the total number of years lost, these individuals were systematically denied the freedom to do the things that most Americans take for granted. Not because they gave up that right, as is the case with so many people we have profiled in this book, but because the system failed them.

In addition to their own lives, collectively, families and communities have been denied fathers and husbands and sons. And, regardless of the actual innocence of the wrongly incarcerated father or mother, we can assume that for those who did leave children behind, these children suffer from the same risks that all children of incarcerated parents face, including increased likelihood for being incarcerated themselves. (See chapter 5 for a lengthy discussion of the impact of incarceration on children.)

As a community the wrongful conviction of just these 251 individuals amounts to seven million hours of lost work, $42 million dollars in lost wages, and the $87 million dollars used to incarcerate these individuals who were factually innocent. Finally, and very importantly, we also see the delay of true justice for the victims of the crimes for which these men and women were wrongly incarcerated. For example, in the case of Darryl Hunt, whom we will profile later, he was tried twice and sought a third trial during his nearly twenty years of being incarcerated. This is typical in exoneration cases because they are often riddled with errors and suspicions that result in a judge granting a new trial. Whereas this is helpful to the exoneree as he or she may ultimately be able to prove their innocence in this manner, it is devastating for the victims' families, who have to relive the traumatic events of the crime, and, if they are still alive, for the victims, who are often required to testify in multiple trials across multiple decades. In the case of Ronald Cotton, the victim, Jennifer Thompson Cannino, talks of the trauma of having to relieve the minute details of her rape in the courtroom not once but twice as Mr. Cotton sought justice. Cotton was eventually exonerated through DNA analysis as well, but like so many others, Cotton did not find justice in a courtroom but rather as a result of post-conviction DNA. In the cases of Darryl Hunt, Kirk Bloodsworth, Ronald Cotton, and so many others, while an innocent man was incarcerated the real rapist, child molester, and killer was free to roam the streets and commit other acts of violence. It is impossible to know how many other crimes were committed by the actual perpetrators, but in 104 of the 251 cases of exoneration the actual perpetrator was identified and in the majority of these he was linked to additional crimes that occurred while the innocent person was locked up. Whether we are sympathetic to the person wrongfully convicted or not, the costs to our society are great. And perhaps the greatest is the threat to public safety that we all live with when the real perpetrator is free to roam our communities raping our mothers and sisters, molesting our daughters, and murdering our loved ones.

Exoneration: The Role of DNA

We cannot underestimate the impact of the role that the science of DNA has played in exonerations; in fact *all* of the 251 exonerations to date have been gained at least in part through DNA analysis. That said, DNA is not the miracle cure-all we would like to believe it is.

First of all, DNA is present, collected, and analyzed primarily in murder and rape cases. And, though these are perhaps the two most serious personal crimes, this limitation significantly shapes exoneration. Specifically, because DNA is not routinely collected and analyzed when other crimes occur—assault, robbery, or nonviolent property or drug crimes—when innocent people are incarcerated for these crimes they seldom have any avenue for seeking exoneration. And this is borne out in the data. Though in many cases an exoneree was charged and convicted of more than one crime, for example, Kirk Bloodsworth was convicted of murder, rape, and assault, of the 251 cases there are 69 murder convictions, 48 sexual assault convictions, and 139 rape convictions. In contrast, there are no cases where the charges were limited to drug convictions or nonviolent property crimes.

Estimating the rate of actual innocence and wrongful conviction is also difficult because in fewer than 25 percent of the cases is there biological evidence that can be tested using DNA analysis. As a result, we have no idea about the rate of innocence for crimes like assault, robbery, and drug use and abuse, which seldom include biological evidence. Thus, it's not surprising that the vast majority, more than 95 percent of exonerations, are for the crimes of rape and murder, where biological evidence is often available for analysis.

Second, in research conducted by The Innocence Project, it is revealed that a key problem is the unvalidated or improper use of forensic science, a fact confirmed in the recent investigation by the National Academy of Sciences (2009). In fact, in 50 percent of the 251 DNA exonerations the forensic evidence was improperly analyzed or validated. The conclusion then is that even when individuals have access to DNA testing as part of the criminal investigation and trial, there are no assurances that it is properly done. Not only are wrongful convictions a result of this flaw, but also lawyers who are aware of this may counsel their clients *not* to have the DNA testing done because they fear this outcome. This is especially problematic because DNA is believed to reveal the ultimate truth. Thus, a DNA conviction would be nearly impossible to overturn and as a result the risk of having DNA tested when the processes are faulty is great. This may have been the case with William Osburne.[4]

Another problem that occurs over and over again is the lack of access to DNA analysis for most of the incarcerated individuals. Over and over again, in fact we are shocked at the frequency of this, an analysis of the cases of those who were exonerated reveals that the assumption that DNA analysis is available to those facing serious charges or those fighting a wrongful conviction is flat out wrong.[5] This was confirmed by the U.S. Supreme Court ruling in the case of William Osburne (see endnote 4). Justices writing in the case expressed concern that if post-conviction DNA were available to all inmates this would create a backlog in the testing labs and the courts. Those working on the issue of wrongful conviction and exoneration see it differently: "In the majority opinion, the Supreme Court ultimately decided that the finality of a conviction is more important than making sure the right person was convicted" (Ferrero 2009).

Though some exonerees gain access to DNA testing through federal court—according to The Innocence Project the number is less than a dozen of the 251—for many exonerees, only the dedication of their public defenders or the local media who put intense pressure on judges resulted in these men gaining the right to have their DNA analyzed and considered by the court. Thus, even in the types of cases—rape and murder—in which biological evidence is available, we are unable to estimate the actual rate of wrongful conviction because only a small number of individuals are lucky enough to have their DNA examined and analyzed by a system that claims to be in the business of obtaining justice. We will return to a discussion of changes in the laws that provide new opportunities for access to DNA at the end of the chapter.

Exonerations: Race and Gender

The demographic breakdown of the exonerated population is compelling because it varies so distinctly from the actual incarcerated population. Of 251 exonerees only 3 have been women—and in all of these cases the women were accessories to crimes, not the primary perpetrator. Though women make up only about 10 percent of the incarcerated population, if all else were equal we would expect at least 10 percent or twenty-five exonerees to be female. How can we account for the huge gender disparity in exonerations? As noted previously, see chapter 5 in particular, the majority of women go to prison for drug offenses and nonviolent property crime. And, as we noted above, there is seldom biological evidence available for analysis in drug or property crimes. Thus, though there are likely women in prison who are innocent, they are less likely to be identified because women by and large don't commit the crimes that avail themselves to DNA testing and thus their cases don't contain the types of evidence that can be used to convince a judge to revisit a conviction.

Sociologically, exonerations are interesting because they come from this very small pool of 251 cases, which forms a tight population for analysis. One of the problems with conducting analysis on the population of exonerees is that quite often there is limited information about the variables that sociologists are most interested in, such as race. Though in the majority of the cases we know the race of the exoneree, it is often difficult to identify the race of the victim. Why? Primarily because of the kinds of confidentially issues that surround rape, the most common crime for which men are exonerated. Unless the victim is murdered, her identity, including her race, is often confidential.

That said, we have solid, reliable race data[6] for the perpetrator in 150 of the 247 exonerations (63 percent) and we have reliable race data for *both* the victim and the offender in 87 of the 251 exonerations (36 percent).

One of the most interesting things about the data on exonerees is the role that race plays in wrongful conviction and exoneration. We begin the analysis by looking at the race of the individuals who were exonerated.

As the data in figure 7.1 demonstrate, African American men are disproportionately represented among the population of exonerees; in fact of the 150 cases in which we have reliable race data for the offender, 105, or 70 percent, are African American.

Clearly there is no simple explanation for such distinct racial differences as there are with regards to gender. Furthermore, though African Americans are disproportionately among the incarcerated population—they comprise about 40 to 50 percent—African Americans men account for 70 percent of the exonerees. The data in the figure indicate that the relationship between race and exoneration is disproportionate and statistically significant. Thus, the claim that it makes sense that African American men make up the *majority* of the exonerees, though true, does not explain the extreme disproportion that is evident in these data.

Given the strong relationship displayed in figure 7.1 we examined the rates of exoneration for African American men taking in to consideration their disproportionate likelihood of being incarcerated. The data in figure 7.2 demonstrate this relationship. As the reader can see, the rate of exoneration for African American men is clearly and statistically significantly greater than the overall rate of incarceration for this same population. Clearly, when we incarcerate 2.3 million people, mistakes will be made. But, if the mistakes are *random* they will be distributed in a pattern that is similar to the phenomenon

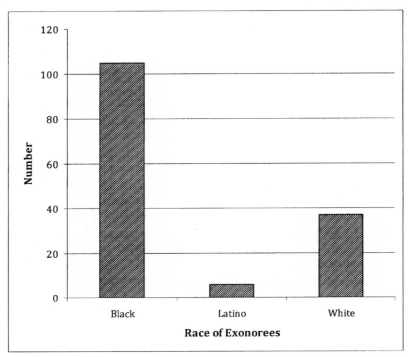

FIGURE 7.1
Race of Exonorees

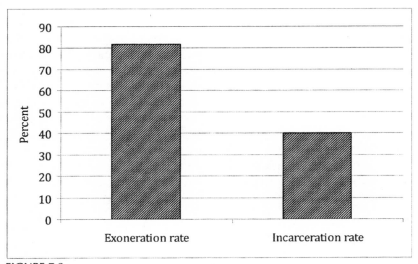

FIGURE 7.2
Ratio of Incarceration to Exoneration for African American Men

itself. In other words, patterns in exoneration would mimic patterns in arrest, conviction, and incarceration. Whenever a phenomenon exhibits patterns that are different than those that exist in the population—in this case the population of incarcerated people as illustrated in figure 7.2—then we have reason to suspect that something systematic and non-random is at work.

The data in figure 7.3 include the rates of incarceration as compared to exoneration for both White and African American men. When we compare these ratios side-by-side, the picture that emerges is disturbing. African American and White men have reverse experiences; African American men make up far more of the exonerated population than they do the incarcerated population. For White men the trend is the opposite, they make up significantly fewer of the exonerations than their overall representation among those incarcerated. This suggests that African American men are disproportionately among the wrongly convicted. The question is why?

When we examine the relationship between race and exoneration the patterns become even more profound when we focus our attention on the particular crimes—rape and murder—that produce the vast majority of the exonerations.

Looking first at homicide, the data in figure 7.4 demonstrate two key facts: first, that about equal numbers of African American and White men commit homicide. Second, homicide is an overwhelmingly *intraracial* crime: people murder and are murdered by others in the same race/ethnic group. Though African Americans are slightly more likely to be the perpetrators in interracial homicides, only 11 percent of all homicides are interracial, whereas 89 percent are intraracial.

Next, we look at the data on rape. The data in figure 7.4 demonstrate a similar pattern. First, we note that, contrary to popular myths about African American men (see Angela Davis's 1983 discussion of "The Myth of the Black Rapist" [1983]), White men make up 50 percent of all men incarcerated for the crime of rape or sexual assault. When we examine the patterns inside the data we see that in cases where the victim is a White woman, 50 percent of the time White men are the perpetrators, and in only 16 percent of the cases are African American men the perpetrators. (Those whose race could not be identified by the victim make up the remainder.) When African American women are the victims, nearly half of the time (43 percent) African American men are the perpetrators. Thus, as with homicide, rape is also predominately an *intraracial* crime.

When we look more deeply at exonerations by examining the racial patterns an even more troubling picture emerges.

As the data in figure 7.6 reveal, the overwhelming majority, 84 percent of the eighty-seven cases on which we have race data on both the exoneree and

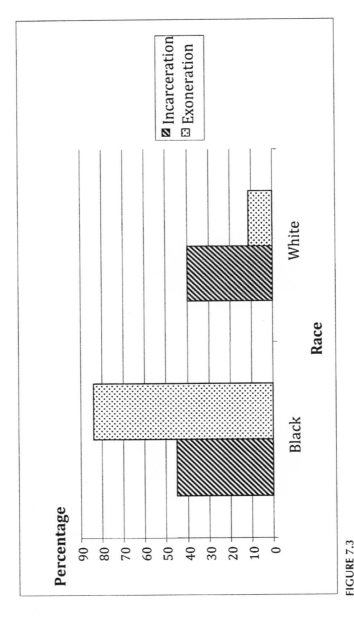

FIGURE 7.3
Ratio of Incarceration to Exoneration by Race

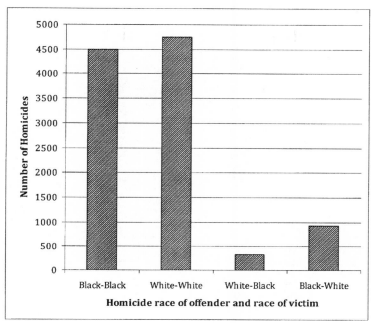

FIGURE 7.4
Racial Composition of Homicide in the United States (2006)

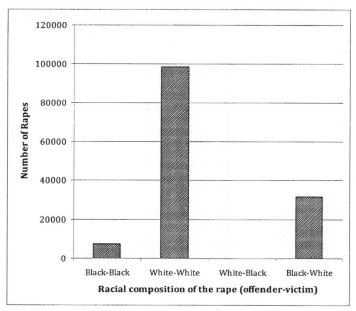

FIGURE 7.5
Racial Composition of Rapes in the United States (2006)

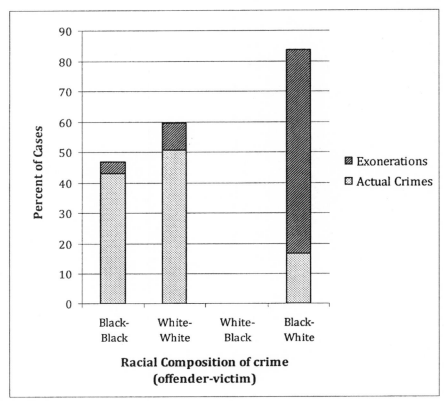

FIGURE 7.6
Ratio of Incarceration to Exoneration by Race and Crime Committed

the victim, involve an African American man being exonerated for the rape and/or murder of a White woman. To put this statistic in perspective, the graph in figure 7.6 compares the racial composition of *actual crimes* and the racial compositions of *exonerations*. As we can see clearly, exonerations follow a pattern that is *exactly the opposite* of the pattern of actual crimes that are committed. African American men commit only 16 percent of the rapes against White women, yet this crime accounts for sixty-eight of the eighty-seven (78 percent) of all exonerations.

It's also interesting to note that when we segregate out crimes in which the victim is only raped (and not murdered), fifty-eight of the eighty-seven (65 percent) exonerations involve a crime that occurs only 16 percent of the time! In other words African American men are four times more likely to be exonerated for raping White women compared to the number of times they actually commit this crime.

As we have noted in other discussions in this book, as important as the statistical evidence is, and in this case the evidence is stunning, often the personal story gleaned from an interview or a set of interviews provides insight into what is behind the numbers. We can be perplexed by the fact that 65 percent of the exonerees are African American men who were wrongly convicted and incarcerated for the rape of a White woman, but the simple statistic can render invisible what this actually means in an individual's life. Thus we would like to share with the reader a portion of the compelling story of just one of the exonerees with whom we have worked: Mr. Darryl Hunt

Exoneration: The Case of Darryl Hunt

The case of Darryl Hunt is, in the words of his attorney Mark Rabil, the quintessential southern crime: Darryl Hunt is an African American man who was accused of the rape and murder of a White woman, Mrs. Deborah Sykes. The case tore at the racial dividing line that is part of the history of Winston-Salem, North Carolina, just as it is in so many southern communities. The aftereffects of the case still reverberate in Winston-Salem and there is still much reconciliation and repair that needs to be done. But, let's get to the story.

On August 11, 1984, a copy editor for the *Winston-Salem Sentinel*, an afternoon newspaper, twenty-six-year-old Deborah Brotherton Sykes was found brutally raped and murdered behind an apartment complex in downtown Winston-Salem. She had been raped and murdered on her way to work in the early morning hours. In September of 1984 Darryl Hunt, a nineteen-year-old African American man, was arrested and charged with the rape and murder. In June of 1985 Darryl Hunt was tried and convicted of rape and first-degree murder. He was sentenced to life in prison.

It has recently been revealed through the pressure of local citizens groups who demanded public access to police documents that there were always some reservations about Hunt's involvement in the case. Long before these documents were revealed, a handful of local residents banded together to advocate for Mr. Hunt and their rabble-rousing generated enough reservation about the case—as well as more witnesses to come forward—that Hunt's attorneys were able to seek a new trial. In May of 1989 Hunt was granted that new trial and in October of 1990 he was convicted again, this time by an *all-white jury* in a neighboring rural county that deliberated just an hour and forty-five minutes. He was again sentenced to life in prison and re-incarcerated.

In 1989 the first DNA exoneration took place and not long after that the popular 1980s talk show hosted by Phil Donahue featured the first exonerees.

Several of the exonerees we have talked to recall watching the episode from their prison cells or dayrooms and glimpsing hope for the first time. Among those lucky enough to win the right to have his DNA tested was Darryl Hunt. Ten years after the murder and rape of Deborah Sykes, in 1994, Mr. Hunt sued for the right to have his DNA tested. The results were conclusive and Mr. Hunt was excluded from the pool of those who could have committed the crime. At the hearing in which Hunt's attorney, Mark Rabil, based on this new DNA evidence pleaded for a third trial, Judge Morgan denied Hunt a new trial based on *his belief that the DNA evidence was not significant enough for either jury to have rendered a different verdict.* In addition, he speculated further that there might be several plausible reasons for the fact that the DNA found in Sykes body was not Hunt's, including the possibility that Hunt murdered Sykes but did not rape her or that he failed to ejaculate when he raped her. By this time, however, prosecutors must have been feeling more and more unsure about Hunt's guilt because they offered him a plea deal: if Hunt would plead guilty to second-degree murder he would be sentenced and released on time already served.

Mr. Hunt had the opportunity to walk out of prison a free man in 1995 but he refused, stating that he would not plead guilty to a crime he did not commit. Discouraged but continuing to believe in his innocence, Hunt's attorneys and supporters realized that the only way to free Mr. Hunt was to find the real perpetrator. By the early twenty-first century, states had begun keeping extensive databases of the DNA of convicted felons and sex offenders in particular. In 2003 Mark Rabil, Hunt's attorney, pleaded with and finally sued for the right to have the DNA from Syke's body tested against the national DNA database. What came back was a near match to a man from Winston-Salem named Mr. Brown. His brother, Willard Brown, was a regular in the Winston-Salem courtroom. He had been cycling in and out of prison since 1977 when he was convicted of robbing a safe. Simultaneously, Mark Rabil attempted to get DNA from Williard Brown who was, in 2003, serving a life sentence under the Three Strikes You're Out law. He had been adjudicated an habitual felon after his most recent arrest in 2002 for drug possession. Rabil met with Brown in prison and offered him a cigarette. Rabil submitted the cigarette for DNA testing and sure enough the DNA sample from Brown matched that taken nearly twenty years earlier from Deborah Sykes's raped and murdered body.

Simultaneously, the local newspaper, the *Winston-Salem Journal*, had been running an investigative report on the Darryl Hunt case. In the process of her research for the eight-part series,[7] reporter Phoebe Zerwick had uncovered police records indicating that early on in their investigation police had briefly considered Brown as a "person of interest" based on the fact that he was the lead suspect in a similar rape that had occurred just two months earlier, in

June of 1984. They quickly ruled Brown out, however, because they believed he had been in prison that summer and therefore could not have committed either rape. Both Zerwick and Rabil checked the actual record and found the error. In the North Carolina Department of Corrections database, Brown's *projected release date* was September 26, 1984. Yet, the record showed he had *actually been released* in late May of 1984 and thus was in the "free world" during the time period in which both rapes were committed. As Rabil points out, even rookie police officers know that the projected release date and the actual release date are seldom the same. Had an officer made the short trip to the county jail in September 1984 he or she would have easily found the actual record of Brown's release.

Finally, on December 24, 2003, after having served eighteen and a half years in prison, the court agreed that there was overwhelming evidence that Mr. Hunt was innocent and he was released from prison. On February 6, 2004, his sentence was vacated and dismissed with prejudice.[8] He was the 152nd person to be exonerated. Mr. Hunt's case illustrates extremely well the problems that lead to wrongful conviction. Thus, his case is worthy of intense study. We will return to this discussion later in the chapter.

Life after Exoneration

Most of us would certainly like to believe that once a person who has been wrongly convicted and wrongly imprisoned for any length of time, but in Mr. Hunt's case for nearly nineteen years, the exoneree would walk back out into the "free world" a truly free person. But, unfortunately, this is seldom the case. Our colleagues Saundra Westerveldt and Kim Cook have been study-ing exonerees. Though their research is still unpublished, in conversations with Professor Westerveldt she reveals that exonerees typically face enormous barriers to reentering society. In her interviews with exonerees, Westerveldt concludes that one of the key struggles many exonerees face is the lingering stigma associated with the horrible crimes of which most of these individuals were convicted. For example, in our conversations with Kirk Bloodsworth, who was convicted in 1985 of the brutal rape and murder of a nine-year-old girl, served a total of eight years in prison, including two years on death row, and was exonerated in 1993, he talked openly about the persecution he con-tinues to face. People have scrawled "child molester" and "baby killer" on his home and his van. Mothers have yanked their young children out of grocery store lines when they realize he is the person standing in front of them. Like so many of the exonerees he has struggled to find employment and to create a personal life that includes a romantic relationship. In short, Kirk served eight years in prison but he has lived with this prejudice and hatred for nearly twice as long.

In Winston-Salem, Darryl Hunt has struggled as well. Because the crime split the community down its racial dividing line, not only must the city adjust to the news that Darryl Hunt did not rape and murder Deborah Sykes, but also racial wounds must be healed. In a poll taken by the *Winston-Salem Journal* in January 2004 after Darryl's release and before his exoneration a *majority* of citizens responding indicated that Mr. Hunt should not be released from prison because they remained convinced that he was in some way connected to the crime. Talk around the water cooler and "official" comments made to Ms. Zerwick via email and phone included comments that "prison was probably good for Darryl Hunt" and "He must still be guilty of something or he never would have been arrested to begin with." Of course, neither of these statements is true. Having worked now for several years with exonerees and learned the intimate details of many of their cases, we have come to believe the only thing we can believe: that this can happen to anyone. And, prison isn't "good" for anyone.

In addition to the specific barriers that exonerees face, they also face many of the same struggles that all reentry felons face including finding a job, reestablishing family life, and generally adjusting to life in the "free world." These struggles are of course exacerbated by the fact that most exonerees went to prison when they were very young—recall the average age was only twenty-six—and they served very long sentences. Not only do they bear the scars incurred from living in such a brutal environment as a state prison—and in some cases on death row—but they also reenter a society that has passed them by.

We offer a "thought" experiment, one that we have often used with students and one that resonates with one of the authors, Angela Hattery. Hattery and Darryl Hunt are roughly the same age. Hattery went to college the same year that Darryl Hunt went to prison. In the nearly twenty years that Hunt was in prison, Hattery went to and graduated from college, earned a master's degree and a PhD, published a book, was appointed to a position as an assistant professor, earned tenure and promotion to associate professor, lived in four states, had two children—who were ten and thirteen when Darryl was exonerated—and has generally lived a very full life. In addition, both authors remember seeing CD players for the first time, using an ATM for the first time, buying their first cell phones, playing a DVD for the first time, and countless other gadgets or services that were developed and released during the twenty years Darryl was incarcerated. In fact, as was brought home again to us in the summer of 2009 when Michael Jackson suddenly died, and we were inundated with Michael Jackson memories, his award-winning album "Thriller" had been released just a year or so before Mr. Hunt went to prison.

This Michael Jackson collective memory seemed like a million years ago to all of us who watched the countless hours of twenty-four-hour cable TV programming, yet the time that passed between the release of "Thriller" and Michael Jackson's untimely death was nearly the length of time Darryl Hunt spent in prison *for a crime he didn't commit.*

If you believe that wrongful conviction and exoneration is nothing more than an unavoidable mistake in a criminal justice system as complex as ours, consider the cases of so many like Mr. Hunt who have the most productive years of their lives taken away from them. We return these individuals to society—often without even an apology—as middle-aged people who languished in prison while life passed them by. They return back to the "free world" behind their peers with regards to occupations and retirement accounts and families never started. They return with twelve or fifteen or twenty-five years missing on their resumes. The return to a world of Blackberrys and iPods; the world they left was populated by Walkmans that held cassette tapes and the first generation of cordless phones. Our "mistakes" rob individuals of years of their lives, years that can never be returned or replaced.

As more and more individuals have been exonerated and more and more social scientists and legal advocates have begun to identify the systematic structures that produce wrongful convictions, exonerees have sought some redress for their experiences through lawsuits that seek monetary compensation. For the early exonerees this process was often extremely lengthy and the outcome was ridiculously unsatisfactory. For example, Ronald Cotton was the first exoneree in the state of North Carolina. When he pursued compensation from the state they initially offered him $500 *per year of his incarceration.* Eventually Mr. Cotton was able to negotiate $10,000 per year, but this is still meager compensation for the years he spent in prison, years that we argued above can never be replaced. Cases like Cotton's, however, have paved the road in two ways for subsequent exonerees: (1) bigger compensation packages and (2) laws that automatically compensate. For example, years later when Mr. Hunt was exonerated he was able to obtain compensation worth nearly twice as much as Mr. Cotton's. His $375,000 settlement, for nearly twenty years in prison, is still remarkably low, but without the precedence set by Mr. Cotton, Mr. Hunt would not have received this much. Secondly, Mr. Hunt was able to receive his compensation in less than six months and thanks to their work and the work of others, it is now a law in North Carolina that exonerees be compensated and that they be compensated at a fixed rate per year. This reduces the work the exoneree has to do in order to receive compensation. North Carolina, however, is one of the most progressive states with regards to exoneree compensation. This may have less to do with the overall nature of the state and more to do with the fact that there have been an unusually high number of cases in North Carolina given the overall incarceration rate. Thus, North Carolina lawmakers were pressured early and often, which is the likely explanation for the law. Other states, like New York, which has the most exonerees in the country, also have exonoree compensation laws but the rules are very rigid and the process to obtain compensation is unnecessarily arduous. For example, though The Innocence Project has identified false confessions as a significant contributor to wrongful conviction, New York law prohibits any exonoree compensation in cases where the individual "contributed in any way to his or her conviction" and that includes falsely confessing, regardless of the circumstances under which the confession was obtained. Thus, our overall analysis is that exonoree compensation has become easier and more appropriate—larger packages—over time, but the situation varies widely from state to state and still relies heavily on the exoneree's own judiciousness as well as the assistance of his or her lawyer and/or the law team at The Innocence Project.

So, what goes so terribly wrong in the criminal justice system to produce cases like Darryl Hunt and Kirk Bloodsworth and Ronald Cotton? Here we review the data that suggest there are several systematic problems that increase the risk of making mistakes that lead to wrongful conviction.

Exoneration: Causes

In short, wrongful convictions—and the exonerations they produce—are a microcosm of the social world, with systems such as capitalism and racial domination playing a substantial role in shaping these patterns. Thus, a careful, systematic, sociological analysis of wrongful convictions and exonerations lays bare one of the most extreme and horrific outcomes of systems of oppression at work in the United States.

We remind the reader to recall the figures that were presented earlier in the chapter. The patterns they illustrate are not only non-random, but also completely outside of the range of normal probability: what we would expect if everything were equal. We offer several explanations that, when taken together, help us to understand this disturbing phenomenon.

(1) *The fallibility of eyewitness testimony.* As the research of others has documented, in 70 percent of the 251 wrongful convictions, the conviction hinged on eyewitness testimony that was later documented to be faulty. Eyewitness misidentification can happen for many reasons. As psychologists have demonstrated using experimental designs even in low-stress situations with relatively long exposures to the "target,"

eyewitness accounts are ridiculously unreliable. In addition these cases force us to examine the issue of cross-race identifications. As noted, the vast majority of the exoneration cases involve a White victim who misidentifies an African American man. In order to better understand this phenomenon, psychologists have performed experiments in which they document that cross-race identifications are significantly harder to make than same-race identifications. This holds even when they use photos of high-profile individuals including actors and professional athletes. There are also a host of specific problems that apply primarily in the criminal justice setting, namely the power that police and prosecutors have to influence memory. For example, in the case of Ronald Cotton, when the victim, Jennifer Thompson Caninno, was shown Cotton's picture the detective in the case reinforced her selection by saying, "We thought so. We thought this was him." Psychologists who study memory note that when a memory is reinforced with both an image (such as a picture) and verbal reinforcement, an individual will begin to replace the original memory images with the image in the photo. Though this may seem preposterous, think about how common it is for us to remember people and places more from the photographs that we have of them rather than the actual people or places themselves. One of the authors has a poignant example. Hattery's grandfather died when her father was only two years old. As an adult, her father, upon careful reflection, realized that what he thought were visual memories of his father were actually visual memories of the photographs of his father that his mother had constantly shown him. If this reprogramming of memory can happen with people we know well and see every day, imagine how likely it is to occur in a crime that lasts only a short period of time and involves people we have never seen before. The case of Ronald Cotton illustrates a further problem. Once the victim, in this case Jennifer Thompson Caninno, has replaced her original visual images with a Polaroid of Ronald Cotton, when she was presented with the physical line-up, she immediately identified Mr. Cotton as her attacker. Not because he was, but because her memory of her attacker is now the Polaroid of Mr. Cotton. Also very reflective, Caninno remarks in an interview with the news program 20–20, which was taped after Cotton's exoneration, that even though she knows Mr. Cotton is innocent and even though she knows the real perpetrator is Mr. Bobby Poole and she knows what he looks like, when she has nightmares about the night Poole raped her and held her hostage in her apartment, she still sees Ronald Cotton's face. In sum, there are several key problems. Identification is harder than it seems. Cross-racial identification is even harder.

And, memory can be shaped by visual and verbal reinforcement such that the reinforcement police officers often give, even subconsciously, and the process of line-ups—photo followed by physical—can lead the creation of a "false" memory.

(2) *The misuse of forensic evidence*: The Innocence Project has carefully catalogued and documented that in 52 percent of the exoneration cases there was improper use of forensic evidence. There are a variety of mistakes that can be made, including failure by the police department to collect and preserve evidence properly, mistakes at the laboratories that conduct the tests (National Academy of Sciences 2009), as well as mistakes in interpretation of the data. For example, countless exonerees were convicted on hair analysis that has been discredited by organizations that regulate forensic science. Yet, prosecutors can always find "hair specialists" who will testify that the evidence is irrefutable.

(3) *False confessions*: Though it is very difficult for most people who have not seen the underbelly of the criminal justice system to imagine, in nearly a quarter (23 percent) of the exoneration cases catalogued and analyzed by The Innocence Project, the wrongly convicted person gave a false confession. How on earth does this happen? There are two different "causes" of a false confession: individual causes and policy causes. In a fair number of cases the false confessions were obtained from individuals who were unable to fully understand the police interrogation. For example, false confessions have been obtained from juveniles who lacked the intellectual development to distinguish between the hypothetical and the actual as well as adults with diminished capacity or mental impairment, who like the juveniles cannot distinguish a story a police officer is painting from the truth. In a variety of cases the common scenario transpires this way. The police officer or detective who is interrogating the suspect asks: "If you were to commit this crime, how would you do it?" The suspect then describes a scenario. The officer then reads the scenario back to the suspect and suggests that in fact this is exactly what happened, that it's not hypothetical but actually the suspect's true behavior. Confused by the difference between the hypothetical scenario and reality, juveniles and those with diminished capacity will then agree to the scenario and the officer will claim that this was a "confession" he or she took from the suspect. A similar variant of this involves telling the suspect all of the details of the crime, offering to write them down, coaching the suspect in what might have happened, and then coercing the subject to "confess" to what has been written down. The second class of false confessions involves people who are not of diminished capacity

but who are convinced by legal interrogation tactics that it is in their best interest to confess. There are so many variants of these that we illustrate with just a few examples. In Darryl Hunt's case, after hours of being detained he was thrown in the "hole" and told that the last "nigger they sent down there didn't make it through the night." He was offered the chance to confess to avoid being thrown in the "hole." Another scenario involves convincing someone that if they confess they will get to go home, typically after hours and hours of grueling interrogation, and that the officer taking the confession will persuade the court to go easy on them. Finally, another scenario involves feeding the individual false information, such as telling a suspect that they have found his (or her) DNA at the scene of the crime, forcing him or her to believe they have actually committed the crime. Exonerees who were "tricked" this way relieve the dissonance between what they think they know and the "evidence" presented by the police officer by constructing explanations such as a black-out or memory loss. These cases are especially difficult for exonerees because for a period of time they actually convince themselves they have committed some horrible crime; remember all the exonerees were convicted of rape and/or homicide. In one case a young man who was only eighteen years old was told by the police that they found his DNA at the scene of the horrific murder of his parents. Though he had no memory of killing his parents—because he hadn't—he confessed based on his belief that the DNA evidence was factual and that he would be sentenced to death. All of these practices of extracting a false confession, taken together, scream for serious revisions to legal interrogation practices. Juveniles and adults with diminished intellectual capacity should be treated very differently by interrogating officers and special care must be taken to be absolutely sure the suspect understands the process and the content of the conversation. Torture and threats of torture should *never* be allowed in police interrogations. Both of these changes to policies require that individual police officers and detectives be trained to recognize cognitive deficiencies and they must be trained with regards to appropriate—not torture—techniques of interrogation. Perhaps most critical is the revision to the laws of interrogation that allow police officers and detectives to lie about evidence. We were absolutely stunned when we learned that this was not just a myth we see presented in countless television shows like *Law and Order*, but that it is legal for police officers and detectives to present suspects with false evidence. We suspect most Americans are not aware of this and we propose that legislation make this practice illegal.

(4) *Snitches*: In more than 15 percent of exonerations an informant or "snitch" was used to testify in such a manner that contributed significantly to a wrongful conviction. The most common scenario involves snitches being paid to testify or testifying in exchange for being released from prison. In most cases the jury is never notified of the exchange—money or time out of prison—that is made for the testimony. Again, this is a practice that must be stopped. Certainly there are cases in which informants have relevant information, and with full disclosure juries and judges should be trusted to distinguish legitimate cases from those that are not.

(5) *The racial history of the United States*: As many scholars have noted, and we have discussed in our own research, the boundary between White and Black sexuality has been the most heavily patrolled and controlled throughout U.S. history (Smith and Hattery 2009). And accusations of the rape of White women by African American men have been a cornerstone of race relations and the justice system for centuries. Angela Davis (1983) documents the fact that the mere accusation of rape of a White woman would send vigilante mobs in search of an African American man to lynch. And more than 10,000 African American men were lynched between 1880 and 1930. Davis documents that only a handful involved an actual rape and a handful more involved consensual relations between White women and African American men. Thus, we argue that the long-standing myth of the Black rapist and the lynching of 10,000 African American men, mostly without cause, provides the historical context, the backdrop if you will, for the way in which the police, the criminal justice system, and even the public deal with African American men accused of rape.

Just as Susan Smith, who deliberately drove her car into a lake in South Carolina, killing her two young sons, whom she had securely strapped in their carseats, blamed a "random" black man, and Charles Stuart, who fatally stabbed his pregnant wife as they left Lamaze class in Boston, told the police a black man had done the stabbing, when African American men are identified as rapists, there seems to be little concern about finding the *right* African American man, the goal is to simply find one, arrest him, and send him to prison. Just as it was during the height of the lynchings, it's as if all Black men are interchangeable. Someone needs to pay for the crime and it's less important that the right Black man be identified than that a Black man pay for the crime. Evidence for this is found in public perceptions about exonoree Darryl Hunt. In the Winston-Salem community it is often noted by Whites that despite Darryl's innocence in the Sykes's murder he probably had done something or he wouldn't have been targeted by the police initially and thus probably deserved the eighteen and a half years he served for other crimes he undoubtedly committed. This perspective, of course, not only suggests the perception that all Black men are interchangeable, but also lessens the guilt of wrongful conviction and exoneration by relying on an assumption that all Black men are engaged in criminal behavior, much of which is probably undetected, and thus time served is most likely time deserved. These assumptions, which permeate some Whites' attitudes about race, are just another vestige of the system of racial domination at work in this country.

Unfortunately there are severe and harsh consequences for this approach to justice. Men like Darryl Hunt, Ronald Cotton, and sixty-eight more whom we have identified have spent, collectively, nearly 1,000 years in prison for raping White women; crimes they, of course, never committed.

Furthermore, in the majority of the sixty-eight cases that involved the rape and/or murder of a White woman by an African American man, locking up the wrong man and allowing the real perpetrator to walk the streets resulted in him being free to commit other rapes and murders. Indeed that is often how the real perpetrators are eventually identified. Though one may say that this is collateral damage for a criminal justice system that ultimately works, that explanation falls short for the women who were raped and didn't have to be and for the families who lost a loved one in a tragedy that could have been avoided.

Lest you not be persuaded by these individual accounts of collateral damage, recall that we noted earlier that most experts suggest that as many as 6 percent, or 140,000, of individuals who are currently incarcerated are *factually innocent* and are the victims of the kinds of problems associated with the criminal justice system that we outline above. When we add to this number the individuals who will be victimized because the real perpetrator is out on the street, we begin to realize that wrongful conviction unnecessarily ruins the lives of an awful lot of people and is in and of itself a threat to public safety.

Exoneration: Solutions

One of the most encouraging things that has come out of the movement around wrongful conviction and exoneration is that the small group of people actively working on these issues is engaged in exactly the type of self-reflection that police departments, prosecutors' offices, and judges should be engaged in. And, as a result of this scrutiny, and the dedication of individuals involved in the movement—including several prominent exonerees—there have been changes made to state laws that should reduce the number of wrongful convictions that are based on systematic errors such as faulty eye-witness testimony.

For example, research on the process of identifying suspects reveals that when the police know who the suspect is in a photo or live line-up they often send intentional and unintentional verbal and nonverbal cues to the victim, signaling her or him to choose the person they have already identified as a suspect. Thus, some jurisdictions have adopted policies that require the implementation of a double-blind design to eliminate this threat to the accuracy of victim identifications. In the double-blind design the officer administering the line-up to the witness does not know if there are any suspects in the line-up or who the suspect might be in either the photographs or among the people recruited for a physical line-up. Similarly, many modifications have been made to the photo line-up process, including a requirement to standardize the pictures used. In the case of Mr. Hunt, his photograph was a Polaroid taken at the station when he was brought in for questioning whereas all the other photographs used in the line-up were mugshots. This type of difference can send cues to the witness that may bias his or her response. Another change involves using sequential rather than simultaneous presentation of photographs in a photo line-up. In many of the exoneration cases that were examined it was demonstrated that when the witness was presented with only one photograph at a time and when she or he did not know the total number of photographs to be viewed the identifications were far more accurate than the "multiple choice" method—where victims are presented with all of the photographs at once and encouraged to "pick one"—that has long been used.

As we noted earlier, the misuse of forensics is another key contributor to wrongful convictions. Repairing this problem involves the training and moderating of forensics at all levels from the local police officer collecting evidence to the lab supervisor running the tests. Clearly resources will be necessary to ensure that this widespread training can be developed and implemented in every jurisdiction in the United States. As these kinds of practices are adopted we suspect the likelihood of wrongful convictions to decrease. Unfortunately, there are no federal laws that mandate these types of changes and in many states there are no policies requiring standardization across jurisdictions. A piecemeal approach like this will likely take much longer to produce a substantial decrease in misidentifications that lead to wrongful convictions. Perhaps as more and more police departments face lawsuits like the one Mr. Hunt brought—and won—in Winston-Salem, North Carolina, the incentive to adopt best practices will increase.

As a result of Mr. Hunt's lawsuit, the city of Winston-Salem commissioned a committee to investigate the Hunt case and learn as much as possible about the mistakes that were made so that recommendations for improving the department could be considered. In their report they found widespread evidence of systematic police misconduct—another cause of wrongful conviction that The Innocence Project reports occurs in about 10 percent of cases. The report found the following:

- By late November 1984, two months after Hunt was arrested, probable cause to believe that he committed the rape and murder no longer existed. Yet, we remind the reader, Mr. Hunt was tried and convicted twice after this.
- Once detectives knew that the blood of Hunt and his friend, Sammy Mitchell, did not match the blood type of the rapist, they conducted little or no investigation to find the rapist.
- By the spring of 1986, detectives should have connected the Sykes case and a February 2, 1985, rape case perpetrated by Willard Brown. Blood evidence in the February 2, 1985, case matched that from the Sykes case.
- Detectives should have more thoroughly investigated two other rapes, one in June 1984, and the other on New Year's Day 1985, to determine if the same rapist committed both crimes and whether that rapist was Sykes's attacker.

These types of systematic procedural errors could have been avoided. How can we understand why they occur in the first place? It is useful to employ the framework provided by Professor Patricia Yancey Martin (2005), who examined police departments, prosecutors, emergency rooms, and judges *as organizations*, in her study of the treatment of rape cases. She argues in this study—and we believe her conclusions can be applied to the case of wrongful conviction—that the heart of the problem lies in the missions of these various offices. In short, as long as the mission of a police department is to arrest someone and "close" the case, and as long as the mission of prosecutors' offices is to send someone to prison and "close" the case and as long as neither office's mission is explicitly the search for truth, we will continue to see the police arrest any Black man who comes close to fitting a victim's description and we will see prosecutors send Black men to prison on very thin evidence. And, when challenged, as they have been in so many exonerations from Roy Brown to Darryl Hunt, we will see them respond by refusing to admit they made mistakes or refusing to allow the truth to be sought by agreeing, for example, to DNA testing. This refusal ultimately prohibits the kind of self-scrutiny that theses offices need to engage in if they are ever going to take the mounting evidence that error is everywhere and deal honestly with the practices in their own departments and offices. Anything short of this severe and widespread overhaul of the criminal justice system means we will continue to engage in the practice of wrongful conviction that damages so many lives and ultimately costs our society tremendously as a result of having to engage in the expensive and lengthy process of exonerations and compensation for exonerees.

And, of course, if for no other reason than this, "getting it right" is the ultimate policy for working to ensure the public safety of all individuals and communities. Each and every wrongful conviction means that the real perpetrator continues to walk the streets, free to continue engaging in serious crimes. And, for a variety of reasons related both to the limited use of DNA and to social factors we explored in this chapter, when the wrong people are incarcerated—almost always for the crimes of rape and/or homicide—the real perpetrators continue to commit rape and to commit homicides. That means that large segments of our population—primarily women and girls who live in the communities where wrongful convictions occur—are vulnerable to becoming victims of some of the most heinous crimes. And in the majority of cases in which individuals have been exonerated, the real perpetrator *did* go on to commit other acts of violence—rape and murder—while the exoneree was wrongly incarcerated (Thompson-Cannino, Cotton, and Torneo 2009).

Exoneration: What the Future Holds

It is encouraging to realize that all of the major areas identified by The Innocence Project—misidentification, false confession, and misuse of forensic science—as contributing to wrongful conviction are being addressed with policy and protocol changes. Yet, as we note, the majority of these changes are taking place at the jurisdictional level and the results are a sort of patchwork quilt that reflects a wide variation in the degree to which any, some, or most of the issues are being addressed in a given area. Until sweeping changes mandated at the federal level are required, systematic errors will continue and so will wrongful convictions. That said, we are optimistic.

It is compelling to think that as DNA analysis continues to be refined and improved it will be the elixir that prevents wrongful convictions from occurring in the first place—which is the ultimate goal of all of those concerned about exoneration.[9] Yet, we argue this is unlikely to be the case. First of all, as noted above, a great deal of expensive and extensive training will be required to bring all the individuals who handle any aspect of forensics—police officers, detectives, lab technicians, and analysts—up to a minimum standard of competence. Second, and perhaps more discouraging, is the fact that the type of biological evidence that is necessary for DNA testing to be done only exists in a very small amount, perhaps 25 percent, of all criminal cases. Thus, in the majority of cases the types of reform we propose above—to police practices, the conducting of line-ups, etc.—will be the *only avenue* that the majority of those who are wrongly convicted will have to see justice served. Finally, we remind the reader that at the time of the writing of this book, in July 2009, the U.S. Supreme Court ruled that once convicted, individuals have no guaranteed right to post-conviction DNA testing (Ferrero 2008). This is perhaps the most discouraging part of the story for it reinforces the finding of Professor Pat Martin when she notes that above all it is the mission of the criminal justice agencies themselves—police departments, prosecutors' offices, and judicial offices—that ultimately deter the search for justice—the very thing they claim is their mission.

Notes

1. "The Trials of Darryl Hunt," HBO Documentary, www.darrylhuntproject.org/trailer.html (accessed on April 5, 2009).

2. The Innocence Project, www.innocenceproject.org/ (accessed on January 12, 2010).

3. The Innocence Project website is also a wonderful clearinghouse for information regarding exoneration itself, including changes in laws, and also provides case summaries for all of the exonerees.

4. Mr. Osborne was convicted of rape in Alaska. In the spring of 2009 the U.S. Supreme Court ruled that he was not legally entitled to have his DNA tested in the case because "Mr. Osborne's trial lawyer decided not to pursue a second kind of DNA testing that was more discriminating. The lawyer said she feared that the results might further incriminate her client. After his conviction, Mr. Osborne sued state officials in federal court seeking access to the DNA evidence for a third kind of yet-more-discriminating testing." Adam Liptak, (June 18, 2009), "Justices Reject Inmate Right to DNA Tests," in *New York Times*. Staff at The Innocence Project, including Peter Neufeld and Barry Scheck, note that this does not necessarily mean that Mr. Osburne is guilty, especially in light of the overwhelming evidence for faulty forensic science. Thus, they continue the fight to allow Mr. Osburne and all Americans to pursue DNA testing and to ensure that access to DNA testing is a constitutionally guaranteed right.

5. Forty-four states have some form of law permitting inmates access to DNA testing. The other six states have no law granting such access. Even in many of the states that grant access to DNA testing, the laws are limited in scope and substance. Motions for testing are often denied, even when a DNA test would undoubtedly confirm guilt or prove innocence and an inmate offers to pay for testing.

6. In addition, it is often unreliable to assign a race to an exoneree unless the photographs are very clear, the name is identifiable, and/or the news reports include racial identifications, for example, "a black man." We eliminated cases in which the exoneree's race was not completely clear or reliable.

7. http://darrylhunt.journalnow.com/.

8. The term "dismissed with prejudice" means that the judge ruled that there was prejudice in his case—mistakes were made—and he can never be tried again.

9. This question was asked by then-Provost Lyle Roelofs at a symposium we organized at Colgate University—the Sio Symposium on Wrongful Conviction and Exoneration—and his question forced us to more carefully explore the proposal that DNA is an "elixir."

8

Where Do We Go from Here?
Policy Implications

R EENTERING THE "FREE WORLD" AFTER MONTHS, years, or even decades of incarceration is one of the most difficult experiences an individual can have. The process is so difficult that nearly 70 percent of the time the attempt is unsuccessful and the individual intent on building a new life finds him or herself returning through the revolving door of prison. Building on the stories of the twenty-five reentry felons we interviewed, this book fills a gap in the research on reentry and recidivism by focusing on the complex and often contradictory process of reentry. Unfortunately, within a year of completing the interviews, two of the individuals whose agonizing stories we were privileged to hear have made that journey back to prison, including one as an habitual felon. Unless there are some drastic changes in the law, he will never see the "free world" again.

Though there are a variety of struggles that reentry felons face, our research revealed several core barriers to reentry beyond those typically identified in the research on recidivism. Moving beyond differences in recidivism that seem to be attributable to race and/or gender as well as the significant and very real impact of low human capital that results in high levels of recidivism, we identified individual and structural factors that enhanced our ability to understand the mechanisms through which individual deficits and structural barriers shape the probability for successful reentry or recidivism. We begin by reviewing these key findings.

Barriers to Reentry

Regardless of variation in the overall experiences and social status locations of the men and women we interviewed, our interviews confirm and provide qualitative support for the two key issues essential to successful reentry that previous research has identified: (1) employment and (2) stable housing. As we discussed in chapter 2, individuals who have a felony conviction face both individual-level discrimination as well as institutional and *institutionalized* discrimination with regards to employment and housing. At the individual level our interviews confirmed what large-scale studies such as Pager's (2003) demonstrate, that regardless of the skills and talents an individual has to offer, when he (or she) checks that mandatory box on a job application that says "I have a felony" few employers are willing to consider him or her for the job. Or, when an applicant for a job in construction is required to demonstrate evidence of certifications in electrical or plumbing, for example, and he is forced to reveal that the certification was earned at a correctional facility, the interview is generally over.

Similarly, especially for those with drug felony convictions—approximately one-third of those exiting prison—and sex offenders, the welfare reforms of the mid-1990s put into place a series of bans that prevent reentry felons from holding certain jobs—such as barbering—and from living in public housing. Additionally, those with drug felony convictions—a status that can be attained from simple possession of five grams of crack-cocaine—are saddled with a lifetime ban on that individual's access to public housing; additional bans include a lifetime ban on receiving cash assistance ("welfare") and food stamps, as well as a lifetime ban on eligibility for student loans. He or she may also face a temporary—often six-month—revocation of his or her driver's license. When taken together, these bans on access to social services and restrictions on employment make reentry through legal means nearly an impossible task, especially for those convicted of a drug felony. Thus, it is not uncommon for reentry felons to quickly return to the "hustle" that got them incarcerated in the first place. With no ability to earn a wage and no place to call home, individuals returning to the "free world," facing seemingly insurmountable barriers, often return to dealing drugs and petty thievery. There is no doubt that these bans and restrictions contribute to the extraordinary high rates of recidivism we see among reentry felons, especially those with drug convictions.

An unexpected finding from our interviews was the cyclical relationship between two "total institutions"—prison and the homeless shelter. Without a paycheck, reentry felons are unable to rent apartments, and with lifetime bans on access to public housing many turn to the network of homeless shelters and soup kitchens for relief. We were frankly stunned by the number of men we interviewed who shared cell blocks in prison and bunk rooms in the local homeless shelters. Certainly their network ties were important in pointing newly released felons toward this network of accessible services, but similarly, this return to familiar networks and living arrangements only exacerbates the problem of recidivism. Those who have been out for a while are quick to provide newly released individuals with information about the homeless shelter, but they are also likely to provide a way back into the hustle. Though there is no doubt that homeless shelters play a critical role in the reentry process—providing shelter for those unable to secure it anywhere else—the movement between one total institution and another contributes to the difficulties reentry felons face in shaking their old connections and habits and learning to adjust to a world in which they not only are responsible for themselves but are also free to make their own decisions. We turn now to a brief review of the additional struggles that "special" populations face as they attempt to successfully reenter the "free world."

Addiction

Without a doubt, untreated addiction was one of the core factors that our subjects identified that contributed to their experiences with unsuccessful—or in a few cases successful—reentry. As a result of the Rockefeller Drug Laws that were initiated in the 1980s, a quarter to a third of the incarcerated population was convicted for simple possession of illegal substances. Prisons are a site where addiction goes untreated, access to drugs is plentiful, and in some cases prisons can be a site for introducing the uninitiated to the use and abuse of drugs. The reader will recall that one of our subjects, Lyman Sykes, reported that he tried drugs for the first time in prison. His first experience with drugs involved experimenting with an inmate concoction that requires "cooking" Tylenol and Benadryl together and injecting the product intravenously. For Lyman, the high was similar to heroin, and once released into the "free world," he immediately began purchasing heroin on the street. Lyman's addiction virtually destroyed his life and he spent at least a decade in prison serving time for his addiction and convictions he incurred that were directly related, such as robbery. Though there were several keys to Lyman's successful reentry, at the core was his ability to become sober and stay sober.

Unfortunately, Lyman's case is unusual. For the vast majority of drug users and junkies we interviewed, their inability to kick the habit resulted in additional barriers to their reentry attempts. Many lived the life of cycling back and forth in and out of prison on possession charges, and, like Lyman, for crimes associated with drug use. And, though only two have returned to prison in the year since we interviewed them, the probability that most will return is high, primarily because there are few affordable, successful treatment programs to which these individuals have access. In fact, on a regular basis as we drive through our community in the neighborhoods near the homeless shelters and treatment centers, it is not uncommon to see men we've interviewed trudging up or down the sidewalk with the dazed look so characteristic of addicts. Without treatment, we suspect we'll soon learn that most of these individuals have returned to prison as repeat drug offenders and parole violators.

Sex Offenders

Another category of reentry felons that face unusual battles are those who exit prison with a felony sex offense. Though it seemed an unlikely probability, among the twenty-three men we interviewed, two, or nearly 10 percent, had felony sex convictions, and two more had convictions for indecent liberties with a minor, for a total of 20 percent of our sample having some sex-related conviction. Both types of offenses require participating in the sex offender registry, though felons have to update their registry more often and for a longer period of time.

Sex offenders face a variety of additional barriers to reentry, not the least of which is the incredibly high rate of recidivism. Recall the story that opens the book: Phillip Garrido kidnapped eleven-year-old Jaycee Dugard within just a few years of being released from prison, where he served only ten years on a fifty-year sentence for the rape and kidnapping of Katie Callaway Hall. The case continues to develop during the time of the writing of this book, and nearly every week, the news reports that there are several other unsolved cases that point toward Mr. Garrido. At its conclusion, it seems likely that the evidence will indicate that Mr. Garrido sexually victimized many young girls and women between his incarceration in the late 1980s and his discovery in 2009. The frighteningly high rate of recidivism among sex offenders is primarily a result of the fact that sex offenders, especially those who commit crimes of pedophilia or ephebophilia, require intensive treatment; only a very small percentage of sex offenders receive any sort of treatment and even fewer are able to secure a place in the relatively rare treatment programs that are moderately successful. This lack of treatment is perhaps the greatest challenge sex offenders face to successful reentry.

The high rate of recidivism among sex offenders should be of great concern to Americans, not only because of cases like Jaycee Dugard or Megan Kanka—for whom the sex offender registry laws are named—but because the average sentence served by sex offenders is three years and two months. Sex offenders serve among the shortest sentences of all felons and they recidivate typically within three years and in the same counties where they were originally arrested. Thus, if we continue to detain sex offenders for such brief periods of incarceration then we must invest in treatment in order to reduce the re-offense and recidivism rates of sex offenders. *It is a simple matter of public safety.*

As noted in chapter 4, sex offenders face additional and unique barriers to reentry. The requirements that Megan's law places upon them require the offender to register his (or her) address regularly with the local sheriff's office and they must live, work, and recreate a specified distance from schools, daycare centers, playgrounds, and many other places children are likely to congregate. These requirements increase the difficulty sex offenders have with securing stable housing and employment. Certainly we do not advocate changing the requirements of Megan's Law, but we do note that these restrictions reduce the likelihood of successful reentry among sex offenders.

Women's Challenges

Among the unique aspects of this book on prisoner reentry, we devoted a separate chapter to the special issues faced by women reentry felons. In general, our approach to studying sociological phenomenon calls for an integrative rather than segregative approach. Our decision to write a separate chapter on women was driven by two key factors: (1) the disproportionately small percentage of the incarcerated population who are women and (2) the unusually distinct challenges that women inmates and reentry felons face compared to their male counterparts.

As noted in chapter 5, whereas many organizations take a "difference" approach to dealing with men and women members, the criminal justice system has taken an almost severely "sameness" approach. As the reader will recall, one of the most critical differences between incarcerated men and women is pregnancy and childbirth. Though many male inmates have medical conditions—both chronic and acute—that require special attention and even transport to a prison specializing in medical care or even a local hospital, the special condition of pregnancy and childbirth puts strains on the criminal justice system and creates unnecessarily inhumane conditions for pregnant inmates. Specifically, pregnant inmates receive spotty pre-natal care and when it is time to deliver they are transported—handcuffed and shackled with leg irons and belly chains—to the hospital where they are forced to endure labor and childbirth while shackled to the hospital bed rails. This puts both mother and baby at risk for medical complications. Shortly after the birth, the child is removed and, if not "claimed" by a family member within twenty-four hours, is taken into custody by the local Department of Social Services and entered into the foster care system. Meanwhile, the mother is returned, less than twenty-four hours after giving birth, to prison.

In addition to the special case posed by pregnancy and childbirth—which affects 6 percent of the female inmate population—the vast majority of incarcerated women (85 percent) are mothers of minor children. The challenges to maintaining contact with her children are a major concern for the inmate mother herself, and research on reentry indicates that it is this contact that is critical to reducing recidivism once she is released. In contrast, though the vast majority of incarcerated men are also parents of minor children, few lived with their children immediately prior to their incarceration. And, though contact between the inmate father and his children is important, the greatest problem children of incarcerated fathers face is the lack of financial support their fathers are able to provide while incarcerated and during reentry. In short, one of the keys to successful reentry is the maintenance of family ties, and the challenges that inmate mothers face are severe, and thus programs must be developed to ease these challenges and thus increase the probability of successful reentry and the reunification of families, which is critical to reducing the intergenerational cycle of incarceration.

Social Capital

As noted throughout the book, our interviews revealed a mechanism by which many can successfully attain both employment and housing and thus increase the likelihood that they will stop the cycle of incarceration that has plagued their lives. This mechanism is social capital. Despite the fact that previous research has demonstrated an interaction effect between race, felony status, and the likelihood of employment (Pager 2003), we identified several African American men with multiple drug felony convictions and decades of time spent behind bars who were able to find *and keep* a job and stable housing. Our analysis revealed that these unlikely-success stories were the result of the ability these men had to access resource-rich social capital networks that others had ignored or were unwilling to access because of the strings attached. Specifically, we learned from Lyman and Linwood, two African American men with fifty years of incarcerated time between them, that the social capital produced by a local reentry program, the Darryl Hunt Project for Freedom and Justice, allowed them to overcome the otherwise insurmountable barriers they faced in obtaining employment and securing housing. In short, the director of the program, Mr. Darryl Hunt, an exoneree, spends a great deal of time building relationships with potential employers and landlords and offers recommendations for reentry felons who are willing to complete a six-week program that includes earning a GED, completing drug and/or alcohol treatment,[1] and taking a series of skill-building classes on parenting, family reunification, resume building, and household finances. When reentry felons complete the programming—the content of which is obviously also critical to their reentry success—Mr. Hunt helps them to secure jobs and stable housing. This finding not only is a reason to be optimistic but also guides our policy recommendations, which we lay out below.

Exoneration

Lastly, we included a chapter on exoneration for several reasons: first, because wrongful conviction and exoneration illustrate in a nutshell all of the problems that plague our criminal justice system in the United States. Additionally, the difficulty that exonerees face with reentry demonstrates that the barriers to reentry are largely structural and institutional and not individual. Consider the facts: exonerees are innocent. Their exoneration is clear and irrefutable evidence that they did not and could not have committed the crime. They are not "bad" people, but rather innocent victims of a criminal justice system less interested in finding the truth and more interested in successfully making arrests, achieving convictions, and closing cases. Yet, just like those who emerge from prison with felony convictions, there are very few exonerees who have been able to secure employment that is not directly related to exoneration itself.[2] Mr. Hunt tells about returning to Winston-Salem, North Carolina, a free man and going around town applying for jobs. Even though he no longer has a felony record—an exoneration removes all charges and convictions related to the wrongful conviction—he has a twenty-year lapse in his work history. He has no references. His human capital has deteriorated. His chances to earn an education have passed him by. *No one will hire him.*

Additionally, exonerees talk about other barriers they face in their reentry process that certainly apply to those who exit prison with a felony record. Chief among these is family reunification. Though most exonerees had strong relationships with their families across their period of incarceration, returning to home and living in the "free world" is challenging for men (and women) who spent decades behind bars. The traits that people in prison develop to keep them safe do not translate well when the expectation is to return to a life of trust and intimacy. And these men were never guilty of anything! Thus, we can extrapolate and infer that for individuals who were guilty, who did commit crimes, and who continue to carry the "demons" associated with those crimes such as an addiction or the scars of being a childhood victim of sexual abuse, reentry into the "free world" and "normal" life are difficult at best and have a high probability of failure at worst. Thus, the exonerees not only lay bare the deep and tragic flaws in our criminal justice system, but also teach us a great deal about the height of the barriers and the depth of the problems reentry felons face. We turn now to a discussion of policy recommendations that come directly out of our research.

Policy Recommendations

As we have noted throughout this book, but especially in the introductory and concluding chapters, successful reentry of previously incarcerated individuals into the "free world" is in all of our best interest for a variety of reasons. First, it is a matter of public safety. When reentry felons slide back into criminal activities, we are their potential new victims. When we engage in efforts to ease their successful transition we reduce the probability that we and our loved ones will be the next victims. Second, incarceration is expensive. Each individual who is incarcerated costs the state or federal government approximately $30,000 per year; a total of $46 billion is spent annually on incarceration. And, these expenses are net losses because the incarcerated individual is contributing little to nothing to the economy in terms of commodities for production.[3] Thus, unlike investments in education or health care, money spent on incarceration is not an investment in anything or anyone. Thirdly, as Americans we profess to believe that everyone deserves a second chance. Presumably when we say that we mean a second chance that is unencumbered by unnecessary barriers to success. We, as a society, owe reentry felons a second chance to become productive and contributing citizens of our society. That said, our proposals for change focus on structural barriers that impede reentry and offer suggestions for some ways in which these structural barriers might be removed, resulting in a greater probability for successful reentry for the previously incarcerated.

Treatment for Addiction

It seems to go without saying, yet it remains a serious issue, that individuals incarcerated for alcohol and drug convictions should be offered appropriate and effective treatment for their addictions. Access to treatment should be open to all who are convicted of drug and alcohol charges as well as those who enter prison on other convictions but who self-identify as needing treatment for an addiction. Unfortunately there are very few effective treatment programs and even fewer beds available within these programs. Though we hear often of famous people like Paris Hilton or Lindsay Lohan going into "rehab" after being arrested for DUI or drug possession, the truth is that the majority of the 450,000 individuals incarcerated for drug and alcohol convictions are never offered a real opportunity to get treatment for their addictions. Additionally, as Lyman's story illustrates, some inmates actually start using and abusing controlled substances while *in prison*. In this case, they enter sober and leave addicted. Because addiction is such a powerful factor in the likelihood of either successfully reentering or recidivating, the development of more effective treatment and its accessibility are critical to reducing recidivism. Without a doubt, it is hard to argue that this would not be money well spent, as our interviews detailed in chapter 3 suggest. Additionally, we would argue that because in-patient drug and alcohol treatment is far less expensive than incarceration, offering first-time drug or alcohol offenders an in-treatment rehabilitation program in lieu of prison would certainly be cost-effective and would likely reduce recidivism among drug felons by breaking the cycle of addiction.

Treatment for Sexual Abuse and Victimization

Just as addicts face additional barriers to reentry that result in unusually high rates of recidivism, untreated sex offenders face similar battles. It seems to go without saying that providing effective treatment for sex offenders is one of the only ways to impact recidivism among this population. Though Megan's Law and its requirements also pose barriers to reentry, and though there is little evidence that the requirements to register and to live and work a certain distance from places frequented by children does much to reduce recidivism, we are reluctant to suggest any amendments to Megan's Law for two reasons: first, because the public believes these requirements reduce sex offenses in their neighborhoods and to amend Megan's Law would cause a public outcry, and second, because the requirements of Megan's Law are not the greatest source of trouble for sex offenders; the lack of treatment is.

Though there are very few treatment programs available for sex offenders, and even fewer that are successful, some research suggests that treatment reduces recidivism from 43 percent to 18 percent.[4] Thus, it seems crystal clear that as with addiction, the key to reducing recidivism among sex offenders is to require the successful completion of mandatory treatment before an individual is eligible for release.

As the reader will recall in chapter 4, sex offenders serve sentences that are significantly shorter than those served by drug offenders. Sex offenders serve, on average, less than three years (33.7 months), compared to mandatory minimum sentences of ten years for drug offenders. And, whereas drug offenders serve 85 percent of their sentences, sex offenders serve, on average, only 43 percent. As noted in the introduction to the book, Garrido served only ten years on a fifty-year sentence for rape and kidnapping. And he offended again within just a few years of his release. Therefore, in addition to mandatory treatment, we propose that sentences for sex offenders be adjusted upward and that sex offenders be required to serve their entire sentence. We remind the reader that the term "recidivism" can sound very mundane, especially in a book such as this where it is used repeatedly. And when we are discussing drug offenders we are primarily talking about returning to drug use and possibly related property crimes that provide access to drugs. When we are discussing sex offenders, recidivism means the sexual abuse, usually of young boys and girls—under the age of thirteen—and is frequently accompanied by kidnapping and, in not such rare cases, even murder of the victims.

We find it remarkable that our society locks up drug users for a decade but releases child molesters after serving fewer than three years in prison. Regardless of one's attitude toward drugs, it is hard to believe that we are more concerned about the impact of drug-related recidivism than sex offenders returning to our neighborhoods, schools, Boy Scout troops, and athletic teams where their presence puts our own children at risk. Perhaps most Americans naïvely believe that their children will never be abused, but with national statistics reporting that one in four girls and one in six boys will be sexually molested by their eighteenth birthday, we need to remove the blinders and take seriously the way we deal with sex offenders.[5]

Address Gender Issues That Matter

There may be many ways in which the process of incarcerating women is no different than the process of incarcerating men. Yet, as we detail in chapter 5, there are specific ways in which women inmates are different from their male counterparts, particularly when it comes to pregnancy, childbirth, and parenting. Anyone working in corrections knows that transporting inmates is risky and is the single action that holds the greatest probability for escape and injury to officers. Thus, the processes for transporting inmates must be carefully developed and implemented. That said, we argue that it is ridiculous to subject a woman in the throes of hard labor to the type of shackling that many women experience as they are transported to the hospital and indeed while they are laboring and giving birth in a hospital bed. Women in hard labor and those in the throes of childbirth do not pose a significant flight risk. Any woman who has given birth knows this. Additionally, the particular shackling practices that laboring women are subjected to put both her and her unborn baby at risk for childbirth-related complications, especially those associated with long labor and labor that is distressed. Thus, we call for these processes to be reviewed and for more reasonable procedures to be developed.

Secondly, the practice of removing the newborn immediately from the mother and allowing her less than twenty-four hours to secure a guardian before the baby is put into the foster care system puts the baby at risk. As Kezia's case illustrated, the process of not allowing women to make a phone call from the hospital alerting their family members that the baby will be born soon or has just been born, and prohibiting them from making that important phone call until they are back in prison, unnecessarily delays the process of transferring guardianship of the newborn from the mother to a relative and in some cases leads to the newborn being put into foster care simply because a relative was unable to appear within the mandated twenty-four-hour period. Children in foster care face significant risks, including lower high school graduation rates, higher rates of sexual and physical abuse, higher rates of delinquency, higher rates of teen pregnancy, and ultimately higher rates of their own incarceration.

Thus, we propose relatively small changes to the procedures—such as allowing the woman to call her relatives when she is transported to the hospital to finish labor and to give birth—which would significantly reduce the percentage of babies who enter the foster care system at the time of their birth. Secondly, we applaud the small number of women's prisons that are experimenting with progressive solutions such as building—or remodeling—facilities that allow for women inmates to keep their babies and toddlers with them—usually until about age two, or creating halfway house–style placements for low-risk inmate mothers of infants and toddlers where they can serve out the remainder of their sentences. We anxiously await the data on these "experiments" as we are optimistic that they will ultimately reduce recidivism among mothers and decrease the likelihood that their own children will enter the revolving door of the criminal justice system.

Create Reentry Programs That Will
Provide Accessible and Viable Social Capital

Based on our research with reentry felons and our work with the Darryl Hunt Project for Freedom and Justice, the data indicate that access to viable social capital significantly reduces recidivism.[6] In fact, as the data in the book demonstrate, access to viable social capital can change the odds of successfully finding employment and thus change the probability of recidivism even for those most likely to be denied employment: African American men with felonies. We are extremely encouraged by this finding, because it offers not only hope, but also practical solutions to the barriers that reentry felons—who are disproportionately likely to be African American men—face. Coupled with a recommendation we have called for before (Hattery and Smith 2007), including the lifting of bans that bar felons, and drug felons in particular, from accessing social welfare programs, we believe that the landscape for reentry could be vastly changed and much improved. And, as noted throughout, lower rates of recidivism mean safer communities.

Thus, we propose that the government provide funding for—but not necessarily oversee—reentry programs that demonstrate that they are successful in assisting with reentry and significantly reducing recidivism. The social capital that is created in these types of reentry programs is relatively inexpensive to fund and it produces reliable and consistent results, especially for reentry felons who have limited access to other sources of social capital, such as families and/or neighborhoods. Additionally, we propose that as a matter of public safety, local governments partner with successful reentry programs. Specifically, once reentry felons complete mandatory training and counseling at a successful reentry program, local governments should agree to hire reentry felons and agree to rent them affordable apartments in public housing units.[7] This type of government support would significantly reduce recidivism and thus contribute to protecting the public safety in local communities. And it is significantly cheaper than re-incarcerating the same people over and over again.

Revamp the Criminal Justice System to Prevent Wrongful Conviction

In the previous chapter we explored the devastating issue of wrongful conviction and exoneration. Wrongful conviction is devastating to the men (and a few women) who spend years and often multiple decades in prison for crimes they didn't commit. But wrongful conviction is also devastating to the public for several reasons: first, because it is expensive. Typically cases that end in exoneration have involved multiple trials, each of which costs taxpayers tens of thousands of dollars in court costs. Additionally, exonerations in most states now carry compensation for the period of incarceration and this compensation can cost anywhere from several hundred thousand dollars to millions of dollars *per exoneration*. Second, because exonerations are typically the result of errors made by police departments and prosecutors' offices, they destroy the public faith in the criminal justice system. Thirdly, and we argue most significantly, wrongful convictions mean that the real perpetrator remains free, often for decades, and in most cases there is evidence that he committed additional rapes and murders. Thus, not only are wrongful convictions an injustice to the individual who spends decades in prison and to the families of the victims and the victims themselves, who often must endure multiple trials, but they are also an injustice to the community because they leave us all vulnerable as potential victims of the real perpetrators.

We propose that each and every institution that is part of the criminal justice system be required, by federal law, to examine its policies and practices in order to identify the kinds of shortcomings and biases that produce wrongful convictions and ultimately exonerations. Additionally, individual agencies and actors need to reconsider their institutional missions, as noted by Martin (2005). Police departments should be rewarded no longer for making an arrest (a collar) and closing a case but rather for *arresting the right perpetrator*. Prosecutors' offices should be rewarded not for securing a conviction but for *securing the right conviction*. And judges should be rewarded not for sentencing, but for *being sure that the process in their courtrooms leads to the discovery of the truth.* Conversely, we suggest that nothing short of sanctions for "getting it wrong" will lead to the types of transformations that will reduce wrongful convictions. Just as Mike NiFong faced criminal charges and was disbarred for his unethical behavior in the Duke Lacrosse case, prosecutors like Tom Keith in Forsyth County, North Carolina, whose office has wrongly convicted at least two and possibly three men who have subsequently been among the 251 exonerated, should face similar sanctions, as should police departments that engage in racial profiling, witness tampering, unethical line-up practices, and other behaviors that lead to wrongful conviction. If there were sanctions for "getting it wrong" and incentives for "getting it right" we suggest that the criminal justice system as a whole would see a reduction in wrongful convictions.

Additionally, we note, based on our extensive analysis of the exoneration data, that the single greatest risk factor for wrongful conviction is race and secondarily gender, in particular the race and gender of the perpetrator and the race and gender of his victim. Overwhelmingly, exonerations involve the rape and/or murder of a White woman by an African American man. Though this configuration accounts for between 10 and 16 percent of these actual crimes, this configuration accounts for nearly 80 percent of exonerations. Thus, racism throughout the criminal justice system—from the police department to the judges' chambers—must be addressed.

Lastly, we are optimistic that this issue is finally being taken seriously, most likely because it is starting to cost taxpayers so much money, and in many states the recommendations of The Innocence Project are being considered and adopted. For example, in North Carolina, new line-up procedures that have been shown experimentally to reduce errors in eyewitness testimony, especially cross-racially, have been adopted and are now mandated in all city and county policing agencies. Many states are considering mandatory access for defendants and even convicts to DNA testing. (We were shocked to learn that this isn't a constitutional right of anyone facing a murder or rape charge.) And reports from the National Academy of Sciences that demonstrate errors in state forensic labs are getting noticed and will likely lead to changes in the ways that state labs process DNA and other forensic evidence. All of these changes are encouraging and will likely reduce the likelihood of wrongful conviction. That said, until the agencies involved at all levels of the criminal justice system reorient themselves toward seeking the truth rather than closing cases or winning convictions, wrongful convictions will continue to plague our system of justice and our communities.

Conclusions

We close this book by asking a simple question: what does all of this mean for the citizens of the United States? Our answer, though complex, rests on a few key principles. First, that our public safety is threatened by high rates of recidivism. When individuals who exit prison are unable to secure the basic necessities of life, primarily employment and stable housing, they are more likely to return to criminal behavior. When they do, we are their next potential victims. Certainly we acknowledge that there will always be individuals who would rather commit crime or who cannot be deterred from it, but we argue here that the vast majority of individuals who commit crimes and are incarcerated for those crimes would rather lead lives inside the boundaries our society has deemed as legitimate than on the margins of illegitimacy. Thus, when it is barriers to successful reentry, not an individual's desire to engage in criminal behavior, that leads to recidivism, we as a society must reduce barriers and create opportunity for successful reentry if we have any desire to reduce crime and overall levels of incarceration in our communities and in our country as a whole.[8] Specifically, removing barriers to reentry, such as bans on living in public housing, and increasing opportunities for successful reentry through providing access to social capital will, in the end, result in safer communities for all of us.

Secondly, incarceration is expensive. The United States spends $46 billion on incarcerating our more than 2.3 million citizens each year. Treatment programs for alcohol and drug addiction and even sex offender treatment programs are far less expensive than incarceration. And, of course, they have the side benefit of reducing the number of potential offenders in our communities, a benefit that is truly desirable especially with regards to sex offenders.

Thus, we would all benefit in terms of dollars saved if our society invested in treatment programs rather than or in addition to incarceration. The long-term benefits would accrue to us all.

Thirdly, reducing recidivism by investing in reentry would likely result in breaking the intergenerational cycle of incarceration. Children who are now at a substantially increased risk for going to prison because they have a parent in prison would likely see that risk reduced if their parent was able to successfully reenter the "free world," become a productive citizen, and invest in their (the child's) social capital, thus increasing his or her likelihood of achieving upward social mobility. Thus, investing in reentry programming is an investment in our future: both our future citizens and our future costs of incarceration.

Though we acknowledge that there will always be a need to incarcerate individuals who pose a long-term and real threat to our society, the fact that our incarceration rate is the highest in the world suggests that things are a "bit out of whack." If we assume these outliers are equally as likely to live in the United States as in any other country, our incarceration rate is disproportionately high because (1) we incarcerate rather than treat and (2) the lack of treatment coupled with institutionalized barriers to reentry result in extraordinarily high rates of recidivism. Reducing structural barriers to recidivism and treating the causes of criminal behavior not only would reduce our overall incarceration rate but would also lead to safer communities for us all.

Notes

1. This is the primary condition or "string" that reentry felons are unwilling to meet in order to gain access to the social capital available in the reentry program.

2. Many exonerees including Darryl Hunt use the proceeds they gain from the wrongful conviction and incarceration to start nonprofits that are generally focused on identifying other wrongfully convicted individuals, providing reentry services for all previously incarcerated people, and changing legislation with regards to exoneration and capital punishment.

3. We address the prison industrial complex in chapter 2. We argue there that millions of dollars of commodities are produced in prisons. Yet, the majority of inmates are not involved in production and thus sit idle all day.

4. Center for Sex Offender Management, www.csom.org/pubs/recidsexof.html.

5. Incidentally, more than 75 percent of all sex offenders are White men. Perhaps this is part of the reason we fail to hold them accountable for their actions.

6. Among the five hundred or so reentry felons who are receiving consistent services at the Darryl Hunt Project only a handful have returned to prison after three

years, a recidivism rate of less than 10 percent, compared to a recidivism rate of nearly 70 percent in the general reentry population.

7. DC Kitchens in Washington, DC, has arranged contracts such as these with the federal government for their trainees in the culinary arts and it has proved very successful. www.dccentralkitchen.org/.

8. We have argued elsewhere that capitalism, and the prison industrial complex in particular, benefits from incarcerating previously unexploitable labor and transforming it into exploitable labor. Thus, the argument that the United States seeks to lower rates of incarceration—even if we hope to reduce crime rates—is therefore debatable. Angela Hattery and Earl Smith, (2008), "Incarceration: A Tool for Racial Segregation and Labor Exploitation," *Race, Gender and Class* 15:79–97.

References

2007b. "Cocaine and Federal Sentencing Policy: Special Report to Congress." U.S. Sentencing Commission, Washington, DC.

Allard, Patricia, and and Lynn D. Lu. *Rebuilding Families, Reclaiming Lives: State Obligations to Children in Foster Care and Their Incarcerated Parents.* New York: Brennan Center for Justice at NYU School of Law, 2006.

Bloom, Alan. "Toward a History of Homelessness." *Journal of Urban History* 31, no. 6 (2005):907–17.

Bloom, B., and D. Steinhart. *Why Punish the Children? A Reappraisal of the Children of Incarcerated Mothers in America.* San Francisco, CA: National Council on Crime and Delinquency, 1993.

Bloom, Barbara, Barbara Owen, and Stephanie Covington. "Women Offenders and the Gendered Effects of Public Policy." *The Review of Policy Research* 21, no. 1 (2004):31–48.

Britton, Dana. *At Work in the Iron Cage: The Prison as Gendered Organization.* New York: New York University Press, 2003.

Browne, Angela. *When Battered Women Kill.* New York: Free Press, 1989.

Bureau of Justice Statistics. 2004. "Special Report: Profile of Jail Inmates, 2002." U.S. Department of Justice, Bureau of Justice Statistics, Washington, DC.

Chang, T., and D. Thompkins. "Corporations Go to Prisons: The Expansion of Corporate Power in the Correctional Industry." *Labor Studies Journal* 27, no. 1 (2002):45–69.

Chasnoff, I. J., H. J. Landress, and M. E. Barrett. "The Prevalence of Illicit-Drug or Alcohol Use during Pregnancy and Discrepancies in Mandatory Reporting in Pinellas County, Florida." *New England Journal of Medicine* 322 (April 26, 1990): 1202–6.

Chen, Te-Ping. "Closing Prison's Revolving Door." *The Nation,* 17 October 2007.

Chesney-Lind, M. "Women in Prison: From Partial Justice to Vengeful Equity." *Corrections Today* 60, no. 7 (1998):66–73.

Colton, M., S. Roberts, and M. Vanstone. "Child Sexual Abusers' Views on Treatment: A Study of Convicted and Imprisoned Adult Male Offenders." *Journal of Child Sexual Abuse* 18, no. 3 (2009):320.

Connell, R., and James Messerschmdt. "Hegemonic Masculinity: Rethinking the Concept." *Gender and Society* 19, no. 6 (2005):829–59.

Davis, Angela. *Women, Race, and Class.* New York: Vintage Books, 1983.

Edin, Kathryn, and Laura Lein. *Making Ends Meet: How Single Mothers Survive Welfare and Low-Wage Work.* New York: Russell Sage Foundation, 1997.

Editorial. "Smarter Sentencing Saves Money." *(Waltham, MA) Metro West Daily News,* 29 November 2009.

Eisenberg, N., R. G. Owens, and M. E. Dewey. "Attitudes of Health Professionals to Child Sexual Abuse and Incest." *Child Abuse and Neglect* 11, no. 1 (1987): 109–16.

Elsner, Alan. *Gates of Injustice: The Crisis in America's Prisons.* New York: Prentice Hall, 2006.

Enos, S. *Mothering from the Inside: Parenting in a Women's Prison.* Albany, NY: State University of New York Press, 2001.

Favro, Tony. "Up to 10 Million American Children Suffer the Consequences of Convicted Parents." City Mayors Society. 2007.

Ferman, Patricia and Louis Ferman. "The Structural Underpinnings of the Irregular Economy." *Poverty and Human Resources Abstracts* 85 (1973):5–17.

Ferrero, Eric. 2008. "U.S. Supreme Court Decision on DNA Testing Is Disappointing But Will Have Limited Impact, Innocence Project Says." The Innocence Project, New York. www.citymayors.com/society/usa-prisoners-children.html (accessed on January 12, 2010).

Finkelhor, David. "Is Child Abuse Overreported: The Data Rebut Arguments for Less Intervention." *Public Welfare* 48 (1990):46–47.

Foster, Holly and John Hagan. "The Mass Incarceration of Parents in America: Issues of Race/Ethnicity, Collateral Damage to Children, and Prisoner Reentry." *ANNALS* 623 (2009):179–94.

Freudenberg, Nicholas, Jessie Daniels, Martha Crum, Tiffany Perkins, and Beth E. Richie. "Coming Home From Jail: The Social and Health Consequences of Community Reentry for Women, Male Adolescents, and Their Families and Communities 10.2105/AJPH.2004.056325." *Am J Public Health* 95 (2005):1725–36.

Friedman, Jaclyn, and Jessica Valenti. *Yes Means Yes: Visions of Female Sexual Power and A World Without Rape.* Berkeley, CA: Seal Press, 2008.

Fritsch, T. A. and J. D. Burkhead. "Behavioral Reactions of Children to Parental Absence Due to Imprisonment." *Family Relations* 30, no. 1 (1981):83–88.

Golden, Renny. *War on the Family: Imprisoned Mothers and the Children They Leave Behind.* New York: Routledge, 2005.

Goodkind, S., I. Ng, and R. C. Sarri. "The Impact of Sexual Abuse in the Lives of Young Women Involved or at Risk of Involvement with the Juvenile Justice System." *Violence Against Women* 12, no. 5 (2006):456–77.

Green, G., P. Leann, M. Tigges, and I. Browne. "Social Resources, Job Search and Poverty in Atlanta." *Research in Community Sociology* 5 (1995):161–82.

Greenfeld, Lawrence A., Tracy L. Snell, and U.S. Bureau of Justice Statistics. 1999. *Women Offenders.* Washington, DC: U.S. Dept. of Justice Office of Justice Programs Bureau of Justice Statistics.

Gross, Samuel. "Convicting the Innocent." *Annual Review of Law and Social Science* 4 (2008):173–79.

Hallett, Michael. "Commerce with Criminals: The New Colonialism in Criminal Justice." *The Review of Policy Research* 21 (2004):49–62.

Haney, Craig, and Philip Zimbardo. "The Past and Future of U.S. Prison Policy: Twenty-five Years after the Stanford Prison Experiment." *American Psychologist* 53 (1998):709–27.

Hanson, R. K. "The Psychological Impact of Sexual Assault on Women and Children: A Review." *Annals of Sex Research* 3 (1990):187–232.

Hanson, S., and G. Pratt. "Job Search and the Occupational Segregation of Women." *Annals of the Association of American Geographers* 81 (1991):229–53.

Harrison, Paige M., and Allen J. Beck. 2004. "Prisoners in 2003." Washington, DC: Bureau of Justice Statistics.

Harrison, Paige M., and Allen J. Beck. 2005. "Prisoners in 2004." Washington, DC: Bureau of Justice Statistics.

Hattery, Angela. "Sexual Abuse in Childhood and Adolescence and Intimate Partner Violence in Adulthood among African American and White Women." *Race, Gender and Class* 15 (2009):79–97.

Hattery, Angela J. *Intimate Partner Violence.* Lanham, MD: Rowman & Littlefield, 2008.

Hattery, Angela, and Earl Smith. *African American Families.* Thousand Oaks, CA: SAGE, 2007a.

Hattery, Angela J., and Earl Smith. "Social Stratification in the New/Old South:The Influences of Racial Segregation on Social Class in the Deep South." *Journal of Poverty Research* 11 (2007b):55–81.

Hattery, Angela, and Earl Smith. "Incarceration: A Tool for Racial Segregation and Labor Exploitation." *Race, Gender and Class* 15 (2008):79–97.

Hibbard, R. A., and T. W. Zollinger. "Patterns of Child Sexual Knowledge among Professionals." *Child Abuse and Neglect* 14 (1990):347–55.

Holmes, W. C., and G. B. Slap. "Sexual Abuse of Boys: Definition, Prevalence, Correlates, Sequelae, and Management." *JAMA* 280 (1998):1855–62.

Islam-Zwart, Kayleen A., and Peter W. Vik. "Female Adjustment to Incarceration as Influenced by Sexual Assault History." *Criminal Justice and Behavior* 31, no. 5 (2004):521–41.

Justice Policy Institute, 2000; www.justicepolicy.org/images/upload/oo-05_REP_PunishingDecade_AC.pdf.

Kimmel, Michael. *Manhood in America* (New York: Oxford University Press, 2005).

King, R., and M. Mauer. "Sentencing with Discretion: Crack Cocaine Sentencing after Booker." Washington, DC: Sentencing Project, 2006. www.sentencingproject.org/doc/publications/dp-sentencing-cc-afterbooker.pdf (accessed on October 11, 2009).

Krisberg, Barry A. and Carolyn Engel Temin. 2001. "The Plight of Children Whose Parents Are in Prison." National Council on Crime and Delinquency. Oakland, CA.

Kurlychek, Megan, Robert Brame, and Shawn Bushway. "Scarlet Letters and Recidivism: Does An Old Criminal Record Predict Future Offending?" *Criminology and Public Policy* 5, no. 3 (2006):483–504.

La Vigne, N. G., R. L. Naser, L. E. Brooks, and J. L. Castro. "Examining the Effect of Incarceration and In-Prison Family Contact on Prisoners' Family Relationships." *Journal of Contemporary Criminal Justice* 21, no. 4 (2005):314–35.

Langan, Patrick A., Erica L. Schmitt, and Matthew R. Durose. 2003. "Recidivism of Sex Offenders Released from Prison in 1994." Washington, DC: Bureau of Justice Statistics.

Lin, N. "Inequality in Social Capital." *Contemporary Sociology* 29, no. 6 (2000):785–95.

Liptak, Adam. "Justices Reject Inmate Right to DNA Tests." *New York Times*, 18 June 2009, A1.

MacMillan, H. L., J. E. Fleming, N. Trocme, M. H. Boyle, M. Wong, Y. A. Racine, W. R. Beardslee, and D. R. Offord. "Prevalence of Child Physical and Sexual Abuse in the Community. Results from the Ontario Health Supplement." *JAMA* 278, no. 2 (1997):131–35.

Martin, Patricia Yancey. *Rape Work: Victims, Gender, and Emotions in Organization and Community Context.* New York: Routledge, 2005.

Marx, Karl. *The Communist Manifesto and Other Writings.* New York: Barnes & Noble, 2005.

Mauer, Marc. *Race to Incarcerate.* New York: New Press, 2001.

———. "Race, Poverty and Felon Disenfranchisement." *Poverty and Race Research Council* 11 (2002):1–2.

———. "Comparative International Rates of Incarceration: An Examination of Causes and Trends." New York: Sentencing Project, 2003. www.sentencingproject.org/doc/publications/incompartive_intl.pdf (accessed on October 11, 2009).

Mauer, Marc, and Meda Chesney-Lind. *Invisible Punishment: The Collateral Consequences of Mass Imprisonment.* New York: New Press, 2002.

McGeehan, Patrick, and Mathew R. Warren. "Job Losses Show Wider Racial Gap in New York." *New York Times*, 12 July 2009, A1.

McGowan, B. G., and K. L. Blumenthal. "My Punish the Children?" Hackensack, NJ: National Council on Crime & Delinquency, 1978.

Meierhoefer, B. S. 1992. "The General Effect of Mandatory Minimum Prison Terms: A Longitudinal Study of Federal Sentences Imposed." Washington, DC: Federal Judicial Center.

Morash, Mary and Pamela J. Schram. *The Prison Experience: Special Issues of Women in Prison.* Prospect Heights, IL: Waveland Press, 2002.

Morash, Merry. *Understanding Gender, Crime and Justice.* Thousand Oaks, CA: Sage, 2006.

Morash, Merry, Timothy Bynum, and Barbara Koonm. 1998. "Women Offenders: Programming Needs and Promising Approaches." Washington, DC: National Institute of Justice.

Mukamal, Debbie. 2004. "After Prisons: Roadblocks to Reentry: A Report on State Legal Barriers Facing People with Criminal Records." Legal Action Center, New York. www./ac.org/roadblocks-to-reentry.

Mumola, Christopher. 2000. *Incarcerated Parents and Their Children.* Washington, DC: U.S. Bureau of Justice Statistics.

Murray, Joseph. "The Cycle of Punishment: Social Exclusion of Prisoners and their Children." *Criminology and Criminal Justice* 7, no. 1 (2007):55–81.

National Academy of Sciences. *Strengthening Forensic Science in the United States: A Path Forward.* Washington, DC: National Academies Press, 2009.

Neuspiel, D.R. "Racism and Perinatal Addiction," *Ethnicity and Disease* 6, no. 1–2 (Winter–Spring, 1996):47–55.

Newman, Jason. 2008. "Stop Revolving Door Justice: How Corrections Systems Can Reduce Recidivism" Progressive Policy Institute. Washington, DC.

O'Brien, Patricia. *Making It in the Free World: Women in Transition from Prison.* Albany: State University of New York Press, 2001.

———. "Maximizing Success for Drug-affected Women after Release from Prison: Examining Access to and Use of Social Services during Reentry." *Women and Criminal Justice* 17, no. 2/3 (2006):95–113.

Odem, M. E. *Delinquent Daughters: Protecting and Policing Adolescent Female Sexuality in the United States, 1885–1920.* Chapel Hill: University of North Carolina Press, 1995.

Padavic, Irene, and Barbara Reskin. *Women and Men at Work.* Thousand Oaks, CA: Pine Forge Press, 2002.

Pager, Devah. "The Mark of a Criminal Record." *American Journal of Sociology* 108, no. 5 (2003):937–75.

———. *Marked: Race, Crime, and Finding Work in an Era of Mass Incarceration.* Chicago: University of Chicago Press, 2007.

Petersilia, Joan. 2000. "When Prisoners Return to the Community: Political, Economic, and Social Consequences." Washington, DC: U.S. Department of Justice Report.

———. *When Prisoners Come Home: Parole and Prisoner Reentry.* New York: Oxford University Press, 2007.

Pipher, M. B. *Reviving Ophelia: Saving the Selves of Adolescent Girls.* New York: Putnam Press, 1994.

Portes, Alejandro. "Social Capital: Its Origins and Applications in Modern Sociology." *Annual Review of Sociology* 24 (1998):1–24.

Portes, Alejandro, and Alex Stepnick. "Unwelcome Immigrants." *American Sociological Review* 50 , no. 4 (1985):493–514.

Prothrow-Stith, Deborah, and Michaele Weissman. *Deadly Consequences.* New York: HarperCollins, 1991.

Putnam, Robert. *Bowling Alone: The Collapse and Revival of American Community.* New York: Simon and Schuster, 2000.

Raphael, Jody. *Listening to Olivia: Violence, Poverty and Prostitution.* Boston: Northeastern University Press, 2004.

Richie, B.E. "Challenges Incarcerated Women Face as They Return to Their Communities: Findings From Life History Interviews." *Crime and Delinquency* 47, no. 3 (2001):368–89.

Roberts, D. "The Social and Moral Cost of Mass Incarceration in African American Communities." *Stanford Law Review* 56, no. 5 (2004):1271–1306.

Rolison, Garry, Kristin A. Bates, Mary Jo Poole, and Michelle Jacob. 2002. "Prisoners of War: Black Female Incarceration at the End of the 1980s." *Social Justice* 29, part 1/2 (2002):131–43.

Rosenmerkel, Sean, Matthew Durose, and Donald Farole, Jr. 2009. "Felony Sentences in State Courts, 2006-Statistical Tables." Washington, DC: Bureau of Justice Statistics.

Ross, T., A. Khashu, and M. Wamsley. "Hard Data on Hard Times: An Empirical Analysis of Maternal Incarceration, Foster Care, and Visitation." New York: Vera Institute of Justice, August 2004.

Rozas, Angela. 2008. "Making Sense of Crime During a Recession Isn't so Clear-cut." *Chicago Tribune*, 3 December 2008.

Schwartz, Charon. 2004. "Rehabilitation vs Incarceration: Non-Violent Women Drug Offenders." *Prisoner Life.* www.prisonerlife.com/articles/articleID=16.cfm (accessed on July 10, 2009).

Scully, Diana. *Understanding Sexual Violence: A Study of Convicted Rapists.* Boston: Unwin Hyman, 1990.

Seattle Times. "A Path to Murder: The Story of Maurice Clemmons." *Seattle Times*, December 6, 2009.

Seccombe, Karen. *So You Think I Drive a Cadillac?: Welfare Recipients' Perspectives on the System and Its Reform.* New York: Allyn and Bacon, 1998.

Shaw, Clifford. *The Jack-Roller: A Delinquint Boy's Own Story.* Chicago: University of Chicago Press, 1930.

Smith, Earl, and Angela Hattery. *Interracial Intimacies: An Examination of Powerful Men and Their Relationships Across the Color Line.* Durham, NC: Carolina Academic Press, 2009.

Sokoloff, Nancy. "The Impact of the Prison Industrial Complex on African American Women." *SOULS* 5, no. 4 (2003): 31–46.

Sykes, Gresham M. *The Society of Captives: A Study of a Maximum Security Prison.* Princeton, NJ: Princeton University Press, 2007.

Terry, Karen J. and Jennifer Tallon. "Child Sexual Abuse: A Review of the Literature." New York: John Jay College of Criminal Justice, 2004.

Thomas, Katie. 2009. "A City Team's Struggle Shows Disparity in Girls' Sports." *New York Times*, 13 June 2009.

Thompson-Cannino, Jennifer, Ronald Cotton, and Erin Torneo. *Picking Cotton: Our Memoir of Injustice and Redemption.* New York: St. Martin's Press, 2009.

Travis, Jeremy. *But They All Come Back.* Washington, DC: Urban Institute Press, 2005.

Travis, Jeremy and Michelle Waul. *Prisoners Once Removed.* Washington, DC: Urban Institute Press, 2003.

Turvey, B. 1996. "Dangerousness: Predicting Recidivism in Violent Sex Offenders." *Knowledge Solutions Library.* www.corpus-delicti.com/danger.html (accessed on November 15, 2009)

Venkatesh, Sudhir Alladi. *Gang Leader for a Day: A Rogue Sociologist Takes to the Streets.* New York: Penguin Press, 2008.

Visher, C., N. LaVigne, and J. Travis. *Returning Home: Understanding the Challenges of Prisoner Reentry (Maryland Pilot Study: Findings from Baltimore)*. Washington, DC: The Urban Institute, 2004.

Wacquant, Loic. "Deadly Symbiosis When Ghetto and Prison Meet and Mesh." *Punishment and Society* 3, no. 1 (2001):95–133.

Wesley, J. K. "Considering the Context of Women's Violence: Gender, Lived Experiences, and Cumulative Victimization." *Feminist Criminology* 1, no. 4 (2006): 303–28.

Western, Bruce. *Punishment and Inequality in America*. New York: Russell Sage Foundation, 2006.

Willis, Roderick. "Women's Re-entry Conference Attracts 200 to Coppin." *Baltimore Afro-American*, December 2, 2005, A9.

Wilson, Franklin D. "Urban Ecology: Urbanization and Systems of Cities." *Annual Review of Sociology* 10 (1984):283–307.

Wilson, K. and Alejandro Portes. 1980. "Immigrant Enclaves: An Analysis of the Labor Market Experiences of Cubans in Miami." *American Journal of Sociology* 86, no. 2 (1980): 295–319.

Wilson, W. J. *The Truly Disadvantaged: The Inner City, the Underclass, and Public Policy*. Chicago: University of Chicago Press, 1987.

———. *When Work Disappears: The World of the New Urban Poor*. New York: Knopf, 1996.

Women in Prison Project. 2006. "Coalition for Women Prisoners: Proposals for Reform." Women in Prison Project, Correctional Association of New York.

Wright, Erik. *Class Counts: Comparative Studies in Class Analysis*. New York: Cambridge University Press, 1997.

Index

About the Authors

Angela J. Hattery is professor of sociology at Wake Forest University. She completed her BA at Carleton College and her PhD at the University of Wisconsin–Madison, before joining the faculty of Wake Forest in 1998. She spent the 2008–2009 academic year at Colgate University as the A. Lindsay O'Connor Professor of American Institutions, Department of Sociology and Anthropology. She teaches classes in and focuses her research on social stratification, gender, family, and race. She is the author of numerous articles, book chapters, and books, including *Interracial Intimacies: An Examination of Powerful Men and Their Relationships Across the Color Line* (with Earl Smith); *Interracial Relationships in the 21st Century* (with Earl Smith); *Intimate Partner Violence* (Rowman & Littlefield, 2008); *Globalization and America: Race, Human Rights, and Inequality* (Rowman & Littlefield, 2008 with Earl Smith and David Embrick); *African American Families* (with Earl Smith) and *Women, Work, and Family: Balancing and Weaving*. Her research for this book arose out of her work with Darryl Hunt and the Darryl Hunt Project for Freedom and Justice.

Earl Smith is the Rubin Distinguished Professor and Director of American Ethnic Studies and professor of sociology at Wake Forest University. He earned his PhD from the University of Connecticut, at Storrs. He spent the 2008–2009 academic year at Colgate University as the Arnold A. Sio Chair of Community and Diversity, Department of Sociology and Anthropology. Before coming to Wake Forest he was a professor at both Washington State University and Pacific Lutheran University where he also served as Chair and

Dean of the Division of Social Sciences. His teaching and research focus on the areas of crime, urbanization, race/ethnicity, stratification and sport. He is the author of dozens of articles and book chapters as well as several books including *Interracial Intimacies: An Examination of Powerful Men and Their Relationships Across the Color Line* (with Angela Hattery); *Interracial Relationships in the 21st Century* (with Angela Hattery); *Globalization and America: Race, Human Rights, and Inequality* (Rowman & Littlefield, 2008 with Angela Hattery and David Embrick); *African American Families* (with Angela Hattery); and *Race, Sport and the American Dream* which won the NASSS (North American Society for the Sociology of Sport) annual book award in 2009. He also served as President of NASSS in 2000–2001. Earl Smith also works with Darryl Hunt and the project assisting with education, reentry, and the release of individuals who have been wrongly convicted.

Breinigsville, PA USA
17 May 2010
238184BV00001B/4/P

9 780739 143896